# JERUSALEM COUNTDOWN

## JOHN HAGEE

FRONT LINE

A STRANG COMPANY

Most Strang Communications/Charisma House/Siloam/FrontLine products are available at special quantity discounts for bulk purchase for sales promotions, premiums, fund-raising, and educational needs. For details, write Strang Communications/Charisma House/Siloam/FrontLine, 600 Rinehart Road, Lake Mary, Florida 32746, or telephone (407) 333-0600.

Jerusalem Countdown by John Hagee
Published by FrontLine
A Strang Company
600 Rinehart Road
Lake Mary, Florida 32746
www.frontlineissues.com

Unless otherwise noted, all Scripture quotations are from the New King James Version of the Bible. Copyright © 1979, 1980, 1982 by Thomas Nelson, Inc., publishers. Used by permission.

Scripture quotations marked KJV are from the King James Version of the Bible.

Scripture quotations marked NAS are from the New American Standard Bible. Copyright © 1960, 1962, 1963, 1968, 1971, 1972, 1973, 1975, 1977 by the Lockman Foundation. Used by permission. (www.Lockman.org)

Scripture quotations marked NIV are from the Holy Bible, New International Version. Copyright © 1973, 1978, 1984, International Bible Society. Used by permission.

Quotations from the Quran are from The Quran Translation, 7th edition, by Abdullah Yusef Ali (Elmhurst, NY: Tahrike Tarsile Quran, Inc., 2001).

Cover design by Judith McKittrick

Library of Congress Cataloging-in-Publication Data
Hagee, John.
   Jerusalem countdown / John Hagee. -- 1st ed.
     p. cm.
   ISBN 1-59185-893-3 (pbk.)
     1. Bible--Prophecies--Jerusalem. 2. Jerusalem in the Bible. 3. Bible
   --Prophecies--Israel. 4. Israel (Christian theology)--Biblical teaching.
   I. Title.
   BS649.J38H35 2006
   236'.9--dc22
                                         2005030113

06 07 08 09 10 — 22 21 20 19 18
Printed in the United States of America

*Lovingly dedicated to Derek Prince:*
*A lover of Israel,*
*A world-class Bible scholar and teacher,*
*A personal spiritual advisor,*
*and*
*A most cherished friend*

# CONTENTS

# INTRODUCTION

*J*ERUSALEM COUNTDOWN IS a page-turning heart-stopper! Using my confidential sources in Israel, information from military experts around the world, and electrifying revelations from Bible prophecy, I will expose this reality: unless the entire world—including America, Israel, and the Middle East—reaches soon a diplomatic and peaceful solution to Iran's nuclear threat, Israel and America will be on a nuclear collision course with Iran!

Let's connect the dots.

Iran is the command post for global Islamic terror. Iran has made it clear to America, Europe, and the United Nations that it intends to join the nuclear club. Iran's president has announced that Iran will share its nuclear power with the Islamic world.

Iran's hatred for America and Israel is without limit. Iran's nuclear program is designed to make Islam a global force and, in my judgment, is as great a threat to democracy as Hitler's Nazis and Lenin's Communism.

The attack on 9/11 proved that Islamic terrorists are willing to use their weapons against America on American soil.

America and Israel will be forced to stop Iran's nuclear production or gamble with the national security of both nations.

Will that attack happen—and when?

What will be the response of Islamic nations if America and Israel bomb Iran's nuclear production sites?

Will Islamic nations join Russia in a military coalition to attack Israel as described by the prophet Ezekiel?

The *Jerusalem Countdown* has begun, and in its aftermath the world will change forever!

# Section 1

# WHERE ARE WE TODAY?

IT IS NEARLY impossible to pick up any nationally syndicated news-paper today or watch any national morning news broadcast without hearing about the escalating unrest and impending conflict in the Middle East. Many of these news stories deal with the conflict between Israel and Iran and the looming threat of Iran's development of nuclear weapons.

This book is being written in the spring and summer of 2005. It's very likely that before this book is published early in 2006, America and the nations of the world will be staggering beneath the realization that Iran, a rogue Islamic terrorist state, has officially joined the nuclear club.

Many view Iran's developing nuclear capabilities as a threat to the world's security as well as to the fragile strategic balance in the Middle East. Despite Iran's protest that its nuclear development program is only for the purpose of civilian power generation, its persistent attempts to acquire nuclear weapons tell a different story. In addition, its evil leaders have publicly declared that they will use violence—any kind and any degree of violence possible—to reach Islam's highest goal: a successful holy war (a jihad) against the United States, the *big Satan*, and Israel, the *small Satan*. To reach that goal, Iran continues to seek the support of terrorist organizations in Iraq, Lebanon, and Palestine—including the support of Osama bin Laden and his Al-Qaeda network of terror.[1]

So what does all this mean to you? To me? To Israel? To America? With this book I hope to make you aware of just how important this escalating conflict is to the world. The rise of terrorism in our world and the emerging crisis in the Middle East between Israel and Iran are part of a much bigger picture—that of God's plan for the future of Israel and the entire world. We are going to discover we are facing a countdown in the Middle East—the Jerusalem Countdown, a battle such as the world has never seen or will ever see again. It is a countdown that will usher in the end of this world.

# 1 THE COMING NUCLEAR COUNTDOWN BETWEEN IRAN AND ISRAEL

T HE FINAL BATTLE for Jerusalem is about to begin. Every day in the media you are watching the gathering storm over the State of Israel. The winds of war are once again about to sweep through the sacred city of Jerusalem. The world is about to discover the power of the God of Abraham, Isaac, and Jacob, the Keeper of Israel, "who...shall neither slumber nor sleep" (Ps. 121:4). His righteous fury will be evident in the defense of Israel.

As we begin the chapter, we are going to take a closer look at Iran, the enemy of Israel. Napoleon Bonaparte, the great conqueror of long ago, has been credited with instructing his armies, "Know your enemy!" I want you to know the evil strategies of destruction this enemy of Israel and the world has planned. We must be prepared to stop this evil enemy in its tracks. There isn't very much time to get it right—the stakes are high, and failure is not an option! Unless we prepare today, tomorrow could dawn with the horrors of an Iranian nuclear strike on Israel—or America.

In the fall of 2004, former prime minister of Israel Benjamin Netanyahu and I sat in my office at Cornerstone Church discussing the geopolitical realities of the Middle East just moments before we were to walk out on the platform and celebrate our annual Night to Honor Israel before a live audience of five thousand Christians and Jews. Television cameras were ready to carry our message to ninety million homes and more than one hundred nations.

I asked the former prime minister where Iran was in its development of nuclear weapons. Mr. Netanyahu candidly admitted that during his administration Israeli intelligence had informed the United States intelligence community that Iran was working on medium- and long-range nuclear missiles that would be capable of hitting London, New York City, and Jerusalem.

Mr. Netanyahu continued with the shocking revelation that the U.S. intelligence community was very skeptical of the Israeli intelligence reports. Later, Israeli intelligence gave photographic proof to the U.S. intelligence community that Russian scientists who made nuclear weapons for the USSR during the Cold War and were now unemployed were helping Iran achieve its dream of developing nuclear weapons.

I responded in amazement, "Can anyone possibly imagine the massive global, economic, and political chaos if three long-range nuclear missiles simultaneously hit New York City and Wall Street, London, and Jerusalem? In one hour, worldwide economic collapse could be accomplished, and Western civilization would be crushed."

If Iran cannot develop the sophisticated delivery system to deliver the long-range nuclear missile, they and other rogue terrorist states certainly will have the capability of producing a dirty nuclear bomb that can be delivered in a suitcase.

Can anyone in their right mind actually believe that the Islamic fanatics presently in charge of the Iranian government would not, as soon as they are available, use these weapons on America, which they call "The Great Satan," and on Israel, the eternal object of fanatical Islamic hatred in the Middle East? The president of Iran, Mahmoud Ahmadinejad, has boldly announced to the world via Fox News that he intends to share Iran's nuclear power to all Islamic nations.

Let's look at what the media around the world have discovered and then compare it to the shocking revelations my sources in Israel have told me.

On February 3, 2004, the *Daily Telegraph* of London, England splashed this headline:

**Confession by the Father of Pakistan's Atomic Bomb: "I've Sold Nuclear Secrets to Libya, Iran and North Korea"**

The article written by Ahmed Rashid confirmed that "the father of Pakistan's atomic bomb has confessed to selling nuclear weapons secrets to some of the world's most notorious 'rogue states.'"[1]

The article by Ahmed reported: "The admission that Abdul Qadeer Khan freely sold nuclear technology to Iran, Libya and North Korea confirms one of America's worst fears—that a close ally in the 'war on terrorism' has turned out to be the secret armourer of its worst foes."[2]

The story continues, confirming the chilling fact that the seventy-year-old Mr. A. Q. Khan told investigators in an eleven-page confession that "he had provided the secrets to other Muslim countries...so they could become nuclear powers and strengthen the Islamic world."[3]

Officials said that Mr. Khan first began to transfer designs, drawings, and components for gas centrifuges to Iran between 1989 and 1991. There is clear evidence that Iran has been seeking to develop nuclear weapons for twenty years.

The *Jerusalem Post* bannered headline of August 5, 2003 bluntly stated:

### Iran Can Produce Nuclear Bomb by 2005

The story confirmed that Iran will have the machinery and materials needed to make a nuclear bomb by 2004 and will have an operative nuclear weapons program by 2005.

According to the *Jerusalem Post*, Iran "has been engaged in a pattern of clandestine activity that has concealed weapons work from International Inspectors. Technology and scientists from Russia, China, North Korea and Pakistan have propelled Iran's nuclear program much closer to producing a bomb than Iraq ever was."[4]

Israel is very aware of this looming threat of nuclear attack from Iran. In his book *Countdown to Crisis*, Kenneth Timmerman writes: "Israeli leaders have been warning that it won't be long. On January 24, 2005, Mossad director Meir Dagan told Israeli parliamentarians that 'by the end of 2005 the Iranians will reach the point of no return from the technological perspective of creating a uranium-enrichment capability.' Once you have that capability," he added, "you are home free."[5]

Vice President Dick Cheney addressed the problem of this looming threat from Iran on Don Imus' radio show on January 20, just before the inauguration. "Iran is right at the top of the administration's list of world trouble spots," he said. If nothing was done about Iran's nuclear weapons program, there was concern that Israel "might well decide to act first" to destroy Iranian nuclear and missile sites and let others "worry about cleaning up the mess afterwards."[6]

In the August 26, 2005, issue of *Executive Intelligence Review*, retired general Paul Vallely, head of the Military Committee of Frank Gaffney's Center for Security Policy and a member of the Iran Policy Committee, said, "We've got to bring the hammer down on Iran."[7]

Vallely states: "We cannot let radical Islam and the Iranians destabilize the Middle East and the world...I know the Israelis are prepared to take very decisive action militarily."[8]

Remember that Israel bombed the nuclear reactor of Iraq in 1981, and the world press rose in unanimous condemnation of the Jewish State, accusing it of gunboat diplomacy. Time has proven Israel did the right thing for the world by destroying Saddam Hussein's ability to manufacture nuclear weapons. When America went to war in Iraq in 1992, during Desert Storm, our troops would have faced nuclear weapons that would have birthed the Battle of Armageddon.

April 13, 2005 the Associated Press released the headline:

### Israel Shares Intel With U.S. on Iran Nukes

Israeli Prime Minister Ariel Sharon pressed the U.S. to threaten Iran with international sanctions, warning Iran was quickly approaching a point of no return in its nuclear program. The White House said it agreed that Iran is pursuing nuclear weapons "under a guise of a civilian program" but wants to continue the current diplomacy strategy to solve the problem.[9]

The story continues with the Israeli newspaper *Yediot Achronot* quoting Prime Minister Ariel Sharon as telling Vice President Cheney: "Iran is very close to the point of no return."

Sharon believes the European effort to curb Iran's nuclear ambitions has been ineffective.

Now that France has failed to vote for the EU Constitution by a large margin, Europe appears weak and divided at a critical moment in history when the world is teetering on the brink of World War III.

A senior Israeli official traveling with Prime Minister Sharon, who were guests at the ranch of President Bush, said: "There has to be immediate action taken against Iran. There is a time limit because Iran will soon reach a technological point of no return. Beyond this point of technological no-return...it will be too late."[10]

In an interview with a defector from Iran's secretive nuclear establishment in Paris on July 13, 2005, *Iran Focus*, a nonprofit news service provider that focuses on events in Iran, Iraq, and the Middle East, asked this question: "How soon will they have the bomb?" The defector replied: "As a physicist with a lot of experience and contacts inside Iran's nuclear establishment, I have no doubt in my mind that the regime in Tehran is not far from the nuclear bomb.... The current leadership in Tehran sees nuclear weapons as an indispensable part of its strategy."[11] When asked how the arrival of the new ultra-conservative President Mahmoud Ahmadinejad changed things, he replied: "Now that you have at the head of the executive branch a former commander of the Revolutionary Guards with a track record as the one Ahmadinejad has, the nuclear weapons programme will receive a great boost."[12]

## THE SIX-STEP PROCEDURE FOR MAKING A NUCLEAR BOMB

Uranium, once enriched, can form the core of a nuclear bomb. But enriching it requires hard-to-acquire technology—and time. The equipment that Mr. Khan, the father of Pakistan's atomic bomb, peddled included centrifuges, which are critical to enrichment. Here's how the process works:

1. *Dig it*—Uranium ore is mined, milled, and soaked with sulfuric acid, leaching out pure uranium.

2. *Crunch it*—Uranium is dried and filtered into a coarse powder called *yellowcake*.

3. *Bake it*—The yellowcake is exposed to fluorine gas and heated to 133° F (56° C), converting it into a gas, uranium hexafluoride.

4. *Spin it*—The gas is pumped into a centrifuge that spins at the speed of sound. As it spins, the heavier U-238 moves toward the outside while the lighter, highly fissionable isotope U-235 collects closer to the center.

> 5. *Spin it again*—The slightly enriched U-235 is fed into another centrifuge, where it is enriched further. It moves down a train of some 1,500 centrifuges. Once it is 20 percent pure, the uranium is considered highly enriched. Only at more than 90 percent purity—which takes about a year—is it weapons grade.
>
> 6. *Squeeze it*—The enriched uranium is converted into a metal powder, uranium oxide, which can be molded into a sphere weighing 35 to 100 pounds (16 to 46 kg) and placed in a weapon.[13]

In an article posted on the *National Review Online* on June 27, 2005, best-selling author Joel C. Rosenberg stated: "I just returned to Washington from two weeks in Israel and Jordan where I met with a number of high-level political, military, and intelligence officials. Across the board, they predicted Iran will reach the 'point of no return' by the beginning of next year. That is, by January 2006—if not before—Iran will finally have the technology, the know-how, and the trained nuclear scientists needed to produce highly enriched uranium."[14]

My sources in Israel support this information. They tell me (April 2005) that Iran is in stage 5 and can have a bomb ready in twelve to eighteen months. That would make Iran's nuclear weapons ready by April 2006 unless international diplomacy prevails.

## IRANIAN RESPONSE

Iran has threatened bloody retaliation if attacked, so the Pentagon's military planners are conducting war games to be prepared for any number of Iranian responses—from attacks on U.S. forces in Iraq to missile strikes on Israel to releasing the Al-Qaeda network to launch a terrorist attack on the United States.

Retired Air Force General Tom McInerney speculated, "I believe they could.... The real question is, will it be a nightmare scenario? Will it be nuclear?"[15]

In a secret policy review, the Bush administration ordered the Pentagon to draft contingency plans for the use of nuclear weapons against at least seven countries, naming not only Russia and the "axis of evil"

(Iran, Iraq, and North Korea), but also China, Libya, and Syria.[16]

In addition, the U.S. Department of Defense has been told to prepare for the possibility that nuclear weapons may be required in some future Arab-Israeli crisis. It is to develop plans for using nuclear weapons to retaliate against chemical or biological attacks, as well as "surprising military developments" of an unspecified nature.[17]

These and a host of other directives, including calls for developing bunker-busting mini-nukes and nuclear weapons that reduce collateral damage, are contained in a still classified document called the *Nuclear Posture Review (NPR)* that was delivered to Congress.[18]

## MAP OF IRAN'S MAJOR NUCLEAR FACILITIES[19]

SOURCES: Associated Press; GlobalSecurity.org; ESRI                    AP

## ISRAELI AIR FORCE GENERAL MAPS OUT
## HOW TO ATTACK REACTORS IN IRAN

Former IAI chief Major General (ret) Eitan Ben-Eliahu has already mapped out the aerial penetration routes for an international attack on Iran. He has also reviewed the suitable armaments to use in such an attack—all this, of course, should the political efforts fail.

Ben-Eliahu addressed a conference on Iran's nuclear program, held at the Strategic Dialogue Center at the Netanya Academic College in April 2005. In his lecture, Ben-Eliahu noted that this issue does not concern Israel alone, as "the political and military response must be carried out with international cooperation and coordination."[20]

The former IAI chief reviewed possible ways to attack Iran, noting: "Contrary to the 1981 bombardment of the reactor in Iraq, which was localized and benefited from total surprise, an aerial operation against Iran is an extremely complex task requiring a wide range of means."[21]

Among other things, Ben-Eliahu spoke of the possibility of an international attack on Iran using cruise missiles, similar to the U.S. attack on Iraq in 1998. The Americans have bombers, some of them stealth aircraft, capable of bombing Iran with precision weapons at little danger to themselves.

The optimal weapon, according to Ben-Eliahu, would be the American GBU 28 bomb, capable of deep ground penetration.

Ben-Eliahu told the Israeli press that he had referred to a possible attack on Iran as an expert on air power, and not as a former Air Force commander, and that his words should therefore not be perceived as part of an Air Force plan. "I spoke of military force based on a coalition, not of the Israel Air Force."[22]

Iran has its own interpretation of the comments made by the former IAI chief. In a clear and unambiguous message, Iranian Chief of Staff Muhammad Salimi stated: "We will deal seriously with all threats (made by) the Israelis and the Americans. The people behind these threats are playing with fire. We warn them against becoming involved in a war of aggression against us."[23]

## IRAN, THE BOMB, AND ISRAEL

On April 17, 2005, Netanya Academic College in Israel conducted the conference at the Strategic Dialogue Center with the topic being, "Multinuclear Middle East—Iran, the Bomb, and Israel."

One of the highlights of this very important conference was a telephone interview between Ronen Bergman, a journalist with *Yediot Achronot* newspaper, and Dr. Manouchehr Ganji, former Iranian Scientist Minister under the shah of Iran before the Islamic Republic of Iran overthrew the shah.

The telephone interview is as follows:

*Ronen Bergman:* "So Dr. Ganji, how far is the Islamic Republic of Iran from obtaining its...first nuclear weapon?"

*Dr. Manouchehr Ganji:* "I really don't think they are very far from obtaining it. They are working very hard secretly, and they have got the infrastructure—so far everybody knows about seven of the centers. So I would give them maximum...maximum in my opinion is going to be about two years."

*Bergman:* "Two years from building its first bomb?"

*Dr. Ganji:* "Yes."

*Bergman:* "Some of the speakers today in this interesting conference had wondered about the motivation of the Islamic Republic in obtaining such a capability. How would you describe this motivation?"

*Dr. Ganji:* "Well first and foremost, the outcome of the past twenty-six years rule by the clerics in Iran is their general belief that there is no Islamic alternative to the society, and the Iranians have found out they want to present an Islamic alternative, but the Iranian people have found out that there is no Islamic alternative to the society's economic, political, and social problems. In Iran today there is the general feeling that the whole pretense to Islamic rule is a big lie, and the tide of public opinion has turned strongly in favor of secularism, even among the top government technocrats, official and high up.

"The clerical regime continues to dabble defiantly in the direction of both terrorism and nuclear arms and long-range missiles. To survive, intelligence regarding the regime's efforts to develop nuclear weapons and long-range missiles abound. By now it is a known fact that ever since the 1980s the mullahs have been after the acquisition of long-range missiles and weapons of mass destruction, which include chemical, biological, and nuclear long-range missiles.

"The regime's top people consider it would make their regime invincible, forcing the United States and others to deal with them on their terms. It's known that North Koreans, Russians, former Soviet States nuclear scientists, nautical engineers, and others have been working in Iran to make its dream come true. With the position of the bomb, the leadership thinks that they can act crazy by blackmailing and deterring the U.S. and its allies and prolonging the life of the regime. Of course, Israel they consider to be the target number one, the so-called Liberation of Islam."

*Bergman:* "So basically you are saying, Dr. Ganji, that the regime in Tehran is trying to obtain this military nuclear capability in order to preserve its own status as ruler of the state."

*Dr. Ganji:* "Absolutely. They have lost most of their credibility inside Iran. A great majority of Iranians are opposing the regime. They know it themselves, and the only way that they can survive, they think, depends on their nuclear capability to prevent others from assisting the people of Iran (who are tired of the horror and brutality of the Islamic religious dictatorship). The regime is extremely unpopular; the general hatred of the regime is a reflected hatred of Iran's supreme leader Ayat Allah Ali Khamenei and his *kahu,* so the regime has no…today, no grassroots.

"The clerics are in charge, and their wish is to have nuclear weapons. They will use the exercise, the so-called principle of *tabi'yeh,* their concoction of an Islamic principle that permits them to lie whenever it's in their interest. They have been constantly lying, and they will lie until they get what they want."

*Bergman:* "What do you think would be the steps taken by the Ayatollahs in Tehran once they have the nuclear capability and the means to deliver it to foreign soil?"

*Dr. Ganji:* "I think they consider their enemy number one to be Israel."[24]

## MY SOURCE IN ISRAEL

I have been going to Israel regularly since 1978 and over the years have developed a network of highly qualified and strategically placed confidential sources that have a very clear and certain focus on critical geopolitical developments in Israel and the Middle East.

The following is a telephone interview with a source known to me and a distinguished Israeli leader close to the development of strategic matters in Israel and the Middle East.

The telephone interview of May 2, 2005 is as follows:

*Pastor Hagee:* "This is Pastor John Hagee in San Antonio."

*Source:* "How are you, Pastor Hagee?"

*Pastor:* "I'm doing well, sir. How are you doing?"

*Source:* "Well, I'm doing fine."

*Pastor:* "Are you in a place where you can talk?"

*Source:* "Yes, I can talk."

*Pastor:* "OK. I just wanted to revisit some of the things that we talked about in our last conversation when you and I were alone in my office. Specifically, what we were talking about was Israel and Iran. And in our conversation, we discussed Iran's progress in making a nuclear bomb. Can you tell me again how many stages there are in the making of that nuclear bomb? You told me originally, but I forgot."

*Source:* "Yes. There are either five or six. It depends, but usually there are five stages. They have estimated that they have about one and a half stages to finish, and this can be done with a year to a year and a half."

*Pastor:* "So they have one and a half stages left to go?"

*Source:* "Yes."

*Pastor:* "About how much time will it take them to get the bomb ready?"

*Source:* "According to estimates (I asked the expert in the field), it is something between a year and a year and a half."

*Pastor:* "OK, twelve to eighteen months..."

13

*Source:* "Experts say two years, but then I don't think that the Western world can take chances and wait for two years."

*Pastor:* "Is Iran further along with the making of this nuclear bomb than America believes?"

*Source:* "I don't know. Last week, Vladimir Putin [Russian president] visited Israel. And he said the Russians could prepare the uranium for the Iranians in a way that it could be used for peaceful purposes only and is restricted from military purposes. But once you get enriched uranium, you cannot guarantee that it will only be used for peaceful purposes. It can be converted to military purposes."

*Pastor:* "So the Russians are helping Iran build this nuclear bomb?"

*Source:* "Not only the Russians, but also the French and Germans. They said that what they are helping can be used only for peace purposes or power purposes. And you know it is so ironic that the Iranian ambassador to the United Nations was interviewed only, I think, two weeks ago on CNN. And he said that Iran had to prepare some nuclear power because we don't know how long our oil wells will be there. But those who understand the volume of oil in Iran admit they have enough oil to last over 130 years.

"So it's also some kind of a foolish, you know, people trying to fool all the world, you know, by saying, 'We do it, because maybe we will not have oil anymore.'"

*Pastor:* "Do your intelligence sources in Israel tell you how many different locations there are in Iran where they're manufacturing this bomb?"

*Source:* "There are six locations, and previously I left you a map the last time I was there."

*Pastor:* "I have the map! [See page 9.] OK, so you're believing that Iran will have the bomb ready in twelve to eighteen months?"

*Source:* "That's correct. That's what I gather from people who have talked to me."

*Pastor:* "Thank you for this information! At this point in time, Israel has no alternative other than to take military action against Iran. Do you believe that Israel will do this, or do you think they will wait on America to take military action as Mr. Sharon has been implying in the media?"

*Source:* "I think that it will be a combination [of Israel and America]. Israel received last week, with top secrecy, blockbuster bombs from the United States. You've never seen bombs that can go that deep."

*Pastor:* "So they're [Israel] getting some of those 5,000-pound, laser-guided blockbusters?"

*Source:* "Exactly."

*Pastor:* "So they got those last week?"

*Source:* "Yes, and what I'm saying to you is 100 percent correct."

*Pastor:* "All right."

*Source:* "When I don't know something, I always tell you I don't know."

*Pastor:* "Sure. What do you think Iran's reaction will be against Israel when this happens?"

*Source:* "Iran has long-range missiles that can reach any place in Israel and any spot in Israel."

The confidential source then discussed with me the development of Israeli Arrow missiles, which he believes have the ability to shoot down incoming Iranian missiles headed for Israeli targets. Then I asked the question we had discussed in a previous conversation.

*Pastor:* "Do you believe that Israel will bomb Iran sometime between April of 2006 and September of 2006?"

*Source:* "I believe so. Pastor, you know more than anybody else that it is not Israel's international obligation to commit national suicide."

*Pastor:* "Yes, I agree."

This ended the meaningful conversation concerning Iran's nuclear bomb progress and the belief of my source of the time certain Israel would be forced to respond to Iran's nuclear threat!

On September 23, 2004, Newhouse News Service writer David Wood released the following information:

Amid growing concern that Israel might launch a pre-emptive strike against Iran's budding nuclear program, the United

States is moving ahead with the transfer to Israel of 5,000 heavy, precision-guided bombs, including 500 "earth-penetrating" 2,000-pound bombs designed for use against underground facilities....

The transfer also includes 2,500 2,000-pound Mark-84 bombs, 500 1,000-pound Mark-83 bombs, 1,500 500-pound Mark-82 bombs and live fuses. All the bombs are being fitted with the Joint Direct Air Munitions (JDAM) kit which uses inertial guidance and beacons from U.S. military Global Positioning Satellites for deadly accuracy.

"That's an arsenal for war," said Joseph Cirincione, senior associate for non-proliferation at the Carnegie Endowment for International Peace in Washington. He said any attack on Iran's nuclear facilities, clustered in three major complexes and dozens of other sites, "wouldn't be a pinprick strike; it would have to be a large-scale military airstrike that would result in large-scale casualties."[25]

## How Does This Affect You?

If Iran's nuclear facilities are attacked, you can be reasonably sure that Iran will counterattack either with nuclear missiles they have available or a series of dirty bombs sold to Al-Qaeda sleeper cells in America waiting for the signal to attack.

If September 11 proved anything . . . it proved America is not immune from attack from our enemies. September 11 also proves, beyond any reasonable doubt, that our enemies are willing to use whatever weapons they have to kill as many of us as possible. The highest honor in Islam is to die a martyr killing Christians and Jews. The one who does this awakes in an Islamic heaven surrounded by seventy virgins.

The UN will send their nuclear teams to Iran and look the other way as long as possible. Why? Because the UN deeply resents the United States for not bowing to its global agenda. The UN is livid with the Bush administration for going to war in Iraq when the United Nations disapproved of that war. America's invasion of Iraq exposed the corruption in the UN with the "food for oil" scam involving the upper echelon of UN leadership.

The UN has labeled *Zionism* as *racism*, which means it has a long-standing documented hatred for Israel.

Remember that this book is being written in April 2005, and several authorities have said Iran is twelve to eighteen months from having the bomb. That makes the date, April through October 2006 as given by my source, a time of great concern for the world.

If Israel attacks, there doubtless will be a vast pan-Arabic Islamic army assembled to attack Israel and attempt to drive the Jews into the Dead Sea. Once again, Jerusalem becomes the target! A casual glance at the geopolitical crisis of the Middle East with rogue terrorist states in possession of nuclear weapons...we are standing on the brink of a nuclear Armageddon.

We are on a countdown to crisis. The coming nuclear showdown with Iran is a certainty. The war of Ezekiel 38–39 could begin before this book gets published. Israel and America must confront Iran's nuclear ability and willingness to destroy Israel with nuclear weapons. For Israel to wait is to risk committing national suicide. The leaders of the Islamic Revolutionary Government of Iran are passionate in their hatred for Israel and America.

No prophetic scripture is more crystal clear than Ezekiel's vivid and specific description of the coming massive war in the Middle East that will sweep the world toward Armageddon. Ezekiel's war as described in chapters 38 and 39 will consist of an Arab coalition of nations led by Russia for the purpose of exterminating the Jews of Israel and controlling the city of Jerusalem. The Russian payoff will be the ability to control the oil-rich Persian Gulf.

The demonstration of that hatred is the election of Iran's radical new president, Mahmoud Ahmadinejad, who has been positively identified by three Americans held in the 1979 seizure of the U.S. Embassy in Iran as one of their interrogators during the hostage crisis. On June 30, 2005, the *Washington Times* reported former hostage retired Army Colonel Charles Scott, 73, saying that he recognized Ahmadinejad as one of his former captors, "...as soon as I saw his picture in the paper. He was one of the top two or three leaders. The new president of Iran is a terrorist."[26]

In the days following the June 30 article, several other former hostages have identified Ahmadinejad as one of their captors during the embassy crisis of 1979. Although there has been controversy about whether or not Ahmadinejad was the person pictured in the photos accompanying the article, even *Aljazeera* has indicated his involvement. On Sunday, June 19, 2005, *Aljazeera* reported:

> As a young student, Ahmadinejad joined an ultraconservative faction of the Office for Strengthening Unity, the radical student group spawned by the 1979 Islamic Revolution and staged the capture of the US Embassy.... According to reports, Ahmadinejad attended planning meetings for the US Embassy takeover and at these meetings lobbied for a simultaneous takeover of the Soviet Embassy.[27]

That is not the only element of Ahmadinejad's terrorist pedigree. Other sources have identified him as the executioner at Evin Prison. Former political prisoners who were in Evin Prison in 1981 have said Ahmadinejad was known to them as *"Tir Khalas Zan,"* literally meaning "he who fires coup de grace."[28] *Aljazeera* has also identified Ahmadinejad as a "former Islamic Revolutionary Guard commander, unabashedly conservative and loyal to Iran's Supreme leader Ayat Allah Ali Khamenei."[29]

In comments following his election, the new president vowed to ignite a worldwide Islamic revolution. "Thanks to the blood of the martyrs, a new Islamic revolution has arisen and the Islamic revolution of 1384 [the current Iranian year] will, if God wills, cut off the roots of injustice in the world," he said. "The wave of the Islamic revolution will soon reach the entire world."[30]

Just weeks after his election, Ahmadinejad, the new president of Iran, addressed a conference in Tehran entitled "A World Without Zionism" and declared that: "The occupation regime of Qods [Jerusalem, or Israel] must be wiped off from the map of the world, and with the help of the Almighty, we shall soon experience a world without America and Zionism, notwithstanding those who doubt." He continued his inflammatory comments by saying, "To those who doubt, to those who ask is it possible, or those who do not believe, I say accomplishment of a world without America and Israel is both possible and feasible."[31]

Ahmadinejad's performance at the conference puts Iran firmly on the path of confrontation. An Iranian analyst told *Asia Times Online:* "The danger of such a radical statesman [Ahmadinejad] is that by knotting religious beliefs with the nuclear issue, it makes for an explosive issue that will explode in the face of all Iranians."[32]

What will be Iran's response to Israel's military attack of their nuclear weapons' plants? How will Syria, Saudi Arabia, Jordan, Egypt, and Libya respond?

If these Arab nations unite their forces under Russia's leadership, which has been helping Iran develop nuclear weapons for several years, the inferno described in Ezekiel 38–39 will explode across the Middle East, plunging the world toward Armageddon.

Iran's new president seems to be escalating the confrontation of Iran's Islamic hard-line factions and policies with Israel's determination for continued self-government and independence. In a June 27, 2005, article in the *Christian Science Monitor*, staff writer Scott Peterson reported: "Critics charge that Ahmadinejad will take Iran back into a Talibanesque dark age, reverse eight years of loosening social rules, and accelerate a collision with the US and the West over nuclear policy and terrorism."[33]

Iran has indicated that it will never again suspend conversion of uranium ore and has rejected a resolution from the UN nuclear agency urging it to stop the conversion of uranium at its atomic plant in Isfahan.[34] Russia has announced "a dramatic expansion of its cooperation with Iran on building nuclear power plants, ignoring Bush administration concerns that the program could help Iran build a nuclear bomb."[35] Although Iran has denied that it is developing nuclear arms, sources indicate that it could have a nuclear bomb ready by early 2006.

All indications are that Iran is moving full-steam ahead to do this. According to a confidential report by the United Nations' nuclear watchdog agency obtained on Friday, September 2, 2005, Iran has produced almost fifteen thousand pounds of the gas used to enrich uranium.[36]

The report said Iran has converted raw uranium into about seven tons of a gas called *uranium hexaflouride*, which can be used to make atomic weapons. Former IAEA nuclear inspector David Albright said in a telephone interview from Washington that the amount would be enough for one atomic bomb.[37]

In response to Iran's position on nuclear power, in an interview for Israeli TV, President George W. Bush said, "All options are on the table. The use of force is the last option for any president. You know we have used force in the recent past to secure our country."[38]

What would a confrontation with the Middle East look like for America? What would happen if America entered the battle zone in defense of Israel? What does the future look like between the Middle East and America? These are questions in the minds of many Americans today, and in the next chapter we will consider some of the possible answers to these questions.

# 2 AN AMERICAN HIROSHIMA?

U.S. OFFICIALS ARE still trying to find a diplomatic resolution over Iran's interest in creating nuclear facilities. "But if diplomacy fails, the Bush administration is forced to consider its military options."[1] In a speech on the war on terrorism at the National Endowment for Democracy in Washington DC on Thursday, October 6, 2005, President Bush likened the ideology of Islamic militants to communism, saying that they were attempting to "...overthrow all moderate governments in the region and establish a radical Islamic empire that spans from Spain to Indonesia." He reiterated: "Against such an enemy, there's only one effective response: We never back down, never give in and never accept anything less than complete victory."[2]

In April 2005, FOX News spoke with two retired generals and a military expert who outlined some of the options America has.

## COVERT ACTION

The Bush administration might send CIA agents or commandos to sabotage Iran's nuclear facilities.

"There were no smoking guns, no fingerprints," said Walter Russell Mead with the Council on Foreign Relations. "We wouldn't be faced with that ugly, ugly choice of, we have a war or they get a weapon."[3]

## NAVAL BLOCKADE

U.S. warships would be sent into the Strait of Hormuz to stop the export of Iranian oil. This would pressure the mullahs to give up enriching uranium and allow intrusive inspections.

One downside is that Iran is OPEC's second largest oil producer, so a blockade could also put a stranglehold on the economies of many U.S. allies. Other potential problems are that it may not work fast

21

enough and it would leave Iran's existing nuclear facilities intact.

"So the question is not whether we could do it. We could. The question is, at what cost?" Mead said.[4]

## SURGICAL STRIKES

U.S. forces could zero in on Iranian nuclear targets, hitting the country's highest-risk sites—such as Bushier, Natanz, Arak, Isfahan, and a dozen or more others—using cruise missiles launched from land or sea.

"We are moving some aircraft carrier groups into the Persian Gulf as we speak," said retired Army Major Gen. Paul Vallely. "They will be positioned to launch any aircraft from the Mediterranean Sea, the Arabian Sea and the Persian Gulf."[5]

Next, F-117 stealth fighter jets could take out a radar system by firing missiles and antiaircraft guns at Isfahan or surface-to-air missiles around the Bushier reactor. B-2 bombers carrying eight 5,000-pound laser-guided bunker busters would hit buried targets like the Natanz enrichment site or the deep tunnels in Isfahan.

Surgical strikes would also aim to hurt Iran's ability to counter-attack while limiting civilian casualties, according to Vallely.

"We're not after the population," he said. "We're not after blowing down bridges anymore. We're trying to disrupt command and control, their ability to use their forces on the ground, their forces in the air, as well as their naval forces. Bring them to their knees early. That's the key."[6]

## ALL-OUT ASSAULT

A huge American military effort, involving hundreds of thousands of troops, would be needed to get "boots on the ground." But the experts FOX News spoke with consider that to be the least likely scenario.

The U.S. military is already stretched thin with its commitments in Afghanistan and Iraq. (Iran is four times the size of Iraq, with almost three times as many people.) A ground war could kill thousands, maybe tens of thousands, and the cost could run well into the billions. And assembling a broad coalition would be even more difficult than it was for the Iraq war.

"For one thing, the British don't sound very willing. And let's face it, without the British, we don't have a coalition," Mead said.[7]

Polls now reflect a significant percentage of the American people are weary with the war in Iraq and want President Bush to give a date certain for our troops to come home. A massive ground assault in Iran is simply not on the radar screen.

Kenneth Timmerman addressed the issue of a full-scale U.S. military strike on Iran in his book *Countdown to Crisis* by stating: "A full-scale U.S. military strike on Iran would be costly, ineffective, and counterproductive. We would probably fail to take out all of Iran's hidden nuclear assets. In addition, U.S. intelligence officials argue in private, we would give the regime a winning argument to mobilize those citizens who might otherwise support pro-democracy forces. Instead we should empower the pro-democracy forces to change the regime. We should do so openly, and as a government policy. But we should support nongovernmental organizations, primarily Iranian, to do the work.... We must help Iranians to create the momentum for nonviolent regime change, before the ticking nuclear clock reaches midnight. And it is almost there."[8]

As America considers the options it has to respond to Iran's threat of nuclear conflict, it seems to me that a preemptive surgical strike is an option America is ready to take. Such a response will have a significant effect on U.S. interests in the Middle East and Iran and around the world.

In an exhaustive report by the Center for Nonproliferation Studies investigating the possible consequences of a preemptive attack by either America or Israel on Iran's nuclear facilities, it was stated:

> In the event of an American or Israeli attack on Iran's nuclear facilities, it is likely that Iran would attempt to take advantage of its extensive list of allies in Iraq to further sour the U.S. occupation and provoke clashes between U.S. troops and Iraqi Shi'a, which may well result in a popular Iraqi Shi'a uprising against the American presence in Iraq. In such an event, American casualties and costs would multiply exponentially as Iraq further disintegrates into Lebanon-style violence. Such developments would prove disastrous for U.S. interests in the Middle East and negate any perceived or actual benefits that may be gained from destroying Iran's nuclear

facilities. The fact is that the strategic usefulness of a successful pre-emptive attack on Iran's nuclear facilities is likely to be shortlived if the United States gets further bogged down in Iraq.[9]

On August 23, 2005, Brigadier General Mohammad Reza Jaafari "vowed that his suicide volunteers will destroy United States' interests all over the world in retaliation to any attempt by the U.S. to hit Iran's nuclear installations."[10] Speaking at a gathering of thousands of volunteers for "martyrdom-seeking operations" from the four major cities in Iran closest to nuclear sites, Jaafari stated:

> If America were to make a mistake and carry out an attack against the sacred state of the Islamic Republic of Iran, we will set fire to its interests all over the world and will not leave it with any escape route....Let the U.S. know that if it starts a war on our soil, a war of attrition against Washington will start immediately and we will destroy all its sensitive spots.[11]

## THE ROADMAP FOR PEACE

Let's talk about the present battle for Jerusalem, which is really the Roadmap for Peace. It began in the fall of 2002, presented by what the media call "The Quartet"—America, Russia, Europe, and the United Nations. There are three stages in this Roadmap for Peace.

The *first stage* of the Roadmap for Peace requires Israel to withdraw from Gaza. You have seen that happen before your eyes on the evening television news.

The *second stage* is that Israel is required to withdraw from the West Bank. The *third stage* is a requirement for Israel to give a portion of Jerusalem to the Arabs as a capital for the new Palestinian state.

Islamic fundamentalists will not honor or abide by any Roadmap for Peace. They are using this Roadmap for Peace as a weapon of war. They want peace with Israel one piece at a time. Now they have Gaza. Next they are asking for the West Bank. And the ultimate plum is the city of Jerusalem, which they will make the capital city for a Palestinian state that will be a terrorist state, whose objective will be the destruction of Israel.

The battle for Jerusalem has already begun. And Israel, desperate for peace, is negotiating itself into the greatest war Israel has ever seen. That war will affect every nation on earth, including America, and will affect every person on Planet Earth.

In world history, peace agreements poorly conceived led to an even greater war. A case in point is the Treaty of Versailles, which ended World War I. When the Treaty of Versailles was written, it was so brutal toward the German people that it created the platform through which Adolf Hitler came to power. Had it been written with an ounce of compassion, Hitler would not have had a possibility of surviving. But that Treaty of Versailles made it possible for the Nazis to come to power in a fanatical revival of nationalism, which produced the Third Reich.

The Roadmap for Peace is an ill-conceived document, one that has Israel giving up Gaza, then the West Bank, and then Jerusalem. It clearly violates the Word of God. How so? Joel 3:2 says, "I will also gather all nations [this includes America], and bring them down to the Valley of Jehoshaphat; and I will enter into judgment with them there on account of My people, My heritage Israel…they have divided up my land."

When America forced Israel to give up Gaza, it was clearly violating Joel 3:2. We are giving the enemies of Israel the high ground in the coming war for Israel's survival. It's time for our national leaders in Washington to stop this madness.

I was invited to Washington DC to meet with Condoleezza Rice and other national leaders concerning this Roadmap. When I asked about Jerusalem, this was the answer I received: "Jerusalem is so controversial. It is so sensitive that it's not even on the table for discussion."

So let's put Jerusalem on the table, because Jerusalem is the City of God. "I [God] have chosen Jerusalem, that My name might be there…in this house and in Jerusalem, which I have chosen…I will put My name forever" (2 Chron. 6:6; 33:7).

Jerusalem is the city mentioned in Scripture 811 times. Jerusalem is the city where Solomon built his temple, which was one of the Seven Wonders of the World. Jerusalem is the city where Jeremiah and Isaiah uttered moral and spiritual principles that shaped the standards of righteousness for the nations of the world.

Let the evangelical Christians of America stand in absolute

solidarity with the State of Israel and demand that our leaders in Washington stop saying, "This [the withdrawal from Gaza] is the beginning of Israel's withdrawal."

Fact: Israel should not give another inch of land to the Palestinians until every terrorist organization operating under the Palestinian covering lay down their weapons of war and prove they are willing to live in peace side by side with the State of Israel. The Palestinians should revise their charter calling for the destruction of Israel. Jerusalem is not to be divided, again, for any reason with anyone regardless of the requirements of the Roadmap for Peace.

## AMERICA AND THE MIDDLE EAST CONFLICT

Now let's look at the coming crisis with Iran. Iran is rapidly developing nuclear weapons to use against Israel and America and is ready to share its nuclear technology with other Islamic nations. The president of Iran, Mahmoud Ahmadinejad, has said on international television, "With respect to the needs of Islamic countries, we are ready to transfer nuclear know-how to these countries."[12] That means every Islamic terrorist organization is going to have the opportunity to use these atomic weapons. Now think about that. That means suitcase bombs could be exploding in several of the major cities of America at the same time. Imagine the chaos and confusion of a dozen Katrinas happening at the same time, created by the devastation of atomic suitcase bombs. Each bomb could kill up to a million people if exploded in a highly populated area like New York City. You say it can't happen. You're exactly wrong. Eugene Habiger, former Executive Chief of Strategic Weapons at the Pentagon, said that an event of nuclear megaterrorism on U.S. soil is "...not a matter of *if* but *when*."[13]

During the 2004 presidential debates, President Bush and Senator Kerry said that nuclear weapons in the hands of terrorists represent the greatest danger facing the American people. While on the campaign trail, Vice President Cheney warned that a nuclear attack by Al-Qaeda appears imminent.[14]

From the private sector, Warren Buffet, who establishes odds against cataclysmic events for major insurance companies, concluded that an imminent nuclear nightmare within the United States is "virtually a certainty."[15]

From the academic community, Dr. Graham Allison, director of Harvard University's Belfer Center for Science and International Affairs, said: "Is nuclear mega-terrorism inevitable? Harvard professors are known for being subtle or ambiguous, but I'll try to be clear. 'Is the worst yet to come?' My answer: 'Bet on it. Yes.'"[16]

When the CIA confiscated records from the computer of Dr. Sultan Bashiruddin Mahmood, former chairman of Pakistan's Atomic Energy Commission, at his bogus charity in Kabul, they discovered evidence from Mahmood's computer that at least one Al-Qaeda nuke had been forward deployed to the United States from Karachi in a cargo container. On October 11, 2001, George Tenet, former CIA director, met with President Bush to inform him that at least two tactical nukes had reached Al-Qaeda operatives in the United States. This news was substantiated by Pakistan's ISI, the CIA, and the FBI.[17]

In addition, Paul L. Williams, a former consultant to the FBI on terrorism, indicates that there is empirical proof that Al-Qaeda possesses nukes. British agents posing as recruits infiltrated Al-Qaeda training camps in Afghanistan in 2000. In another instance, an Al-Qaeda operative was arrested at Ramallah with a tactical nuke strapped to his back. And U.S. military officials discovered a lead canister containing uranium-238 in Kandahar at the outset of Operation Enduring Freedom.[18]

If you are having trouble believing that teams of terrorists maintaining a nuclear weapon in the United States wouldn't be detected, think about this.

Williams reports that there isn't just one team, but at least seven.[19] They are working within mosques and Islamic centers. In the United States, a federal judge will not provide any FBI or law enforcement agent with a warrant to search a mosque of an Islamic center for any reason since such places are listed as "houses of worship."[20]

The seven areas that have been identified are New York, Miami, Houston, Las Vegas, Los Angeles, Chicago, and Washington DC. The attacks will occur simultaneously at the seven sites.

I have on my desk an intelligence report stating that Iran is now developing something that is called an *electromagnetic pulse (EMP)* designed to be used against America in a time of war. In March of this year, the Senate Judiciary Subcommittee on Terrorism Technology and Homeland Security, chaired by Senator John Kyl of Arizona, held a hearing on the electromagnetic pulse threat against America.

Listen up—this is extremely important.

Here's what the EMP does. This electromagnetic blanket does not kill people—it kills electrons. In short, it stops every form of electricity instantly and for months, maybe years.[21] Here's how it could be used against America in warfare.

A fake satellite crossing over America at the height of 280 miles suddenly explodes over the Great Plains of the United States, releasing several pounds of enriched plutonium, blanketing the United States of America with gamma rays. Instantly, in one-billionth of a second, all electrical power is cut off instantly, and cut off for months.

No lights, no refrigeration will work in your home. Every ounce of food you have will rot in your freezer. Your car won't work because it starts with electricity. Trucks won't work, meaning transportation bringing you everything you use will stop. All machinery stops. The radio and the television stations will go off the air. Planes that are in flight will crash because their electronic systems will fail. The missile systems will fail to function. We will cease to be a superpower in one-billionth of a second.

The president cannot communicate with his military people in the field because the phones will not work. America's refineries will shut down. There will be no gas and no oil. The gas at the service station can't be used because those pumps get the gas out of the ground with electricity. Computers won't work, meaning city, state, and government offices will be shut down. There will be a nationwide food and gas shortage within a few days.

You say that can't happen? There are people who are planning it right now. It's not new. It's been talked about for twenty years. Only now, rogue states have the ability to put this weapon to use, and it will happen unless Iran and the "axis of evil" are stopped![22]

Can Iran do it? Our government says yes. North Korea, an ally of Iran, also has that ability. Iran is presently ruled by Islamic fanatics who would be more than willing to use those weapons against

America and Israel. North Korea is ruled by an absolute madman who is reported to be schizophrenic and paranoid.

The *Congressional Report* reads: "Even primitive Scud missiles could be used for this purpose [electronic blankets]. And top U.S. intelligence officials reminded members of Congress that there is a glut of these missiles on the world market. They are currently being bought and sold for about $100,000 apiece."[23]

Now think about that!

This great, magnificent nation that is so technically oriented has created an Achilles' heel—electricity. With one $100,000 missile fired from a used submarine 200 miles offshore, and a few pounds of enriched plutonium exploding over the United States, every form of electricity would stop instantly and for months. In one second, we would be living in the nineteenth century.

Where is the world headed?

What is in the immediate future?

If Iran is not stopped in its quest for nuclear weapons, the Iranians will have them soon—and they will use them against Israel. If Iran is stopped, it will happen through military force. Only America and Israel have that power, because Russia is now helping Iran to develop their nuclear weapons. I believe this military action will lead to Russia bringing together a coalition of Islamic nations to invade Israel. The prophet Ezekiel paints that portrait clearly in Ezekiel chapters 38 and 39. We will look closely at Ezekiel's picture of what is to come in the Middle East in Section 3 of this book.

But first we must take a closer look at what brought us to the point of nuclear conflict and devastating war and destruction between the Jewish people, God's chosen people, and the Islamic world. In the next chapter we will discover that the church must rise up out of spiritual fog and religious deception, and focus with laser-beam intensity on the absolute truth concerning the issue of Islam.

# 3 UNVEILING ISLAM

THERE COMES A time in a nation's history—and there comes a time in the church—when spiritual fogs and religious deception must be removed by a clear, unbiased, passionate pursuit of truth.

America and the church are now in a spiritual fog over the issue of Islam. As mosques appear across the nation from city to city, people are asking, "What do I need to know about Islam?" Islam, once an obscure Middle Eastern religion, has rapidly grown into the second largest religion in the world. There are now more Muslims in the United States than there are members of the Assemblies of God. The population of Iran is approximately 99 percent Muslim, of which approximately 89 percent are Shi'a and 10 percent are Sunni.[1]

What attraction does Islam hold for its followers? What part does it play in shaping the attitudes of nearly one billion people around the world?

On 9/11 when the Islamic terrorists flew their hijacked airliners into the twin towers and the Pentagon, Americans discovered we were at war—a world war against fanatical Islamic terrorists who believe that killing Americans and Jews is the will of Muhammad the Prophet—and the will of God, called *Allah*. In war, when one side understands that it is at war (Islamic terrorist), and the other side thinks that its adversaries are apostles of peace, which side has the advantage?

One of the first questions we must answer is this: Are those who follow the teachings of Muhammad, as found in the Quran, peaceful or violent?

America awakened on 9/11 to horrific scenes on TV of passenger planes deliberately crashing into the World Trade Center and the Pentagon. Stunned disbelief gave way to grief—grief for thousands of children who would go to sleep that night without a father or mother.

Grief for heroic firemen and policemen who dashed into the burning towers to save lives—and stepped into eternity into the arms of God. While we grieved, Palestinians danced for joy in the West Bank!

Who would do such a thing? Why would they do it? They were all Islamics who practiced the teachings of the Quran. Islam not only *condones* violence; it *commands* it. A tree is known by its fruit! The fruit of Islam is fourteen hundred years of violence and bloodshed around the world.

What are Muslims taught to do to the people who resist Islam? The Quran teaches:

> Fight and slay the Pagans wherever you find them, and seize them, beleaguer them, and lie in wait for them in every strategem (of war).
>
> —SURAH 9:5

> The punishment of those who wage war against Allah and His Messenger, and strive with might and main for mischief through the land is: execution, or crucifixion, or the cutting off of hands and feet from opposite sides, or exile from the land: that is their disgrace in this world, and a heavy punishment is theirs in the Hereafter.
>
> —SURAH 5:33

In America, cutting off someone's hand or feet because he would not accept your religion is unthinkable—but the Islamic Bible commands it. Iran's Ayatollah Khomeini declared: "The purest joy in Islam is to kill and to be killed for Allah."[2] Is that *fanaticism*—or simply *being faithful* to the Islamic Bible?

Muhammad, the founder of Islam, slaughtered thousands of people in establishing and spreading Islam. He told his followers: "Who relinquishes his faith, kill him. I have been ordered by Allah to fight with people till they testify there is no god but Allah, and Muhammad is his messenger."

One of the most significant questions being asked in Washington and around the world today is this: Why is it that the Jews and the Arabs can't get together in their disputing over the city of Jerusalem? In this chapter I will show you some of the answers. The most important reason Jews and Arabs cannot get together is not *land*…it is not *money* or *history*. The reason for the continual conflict over the city of Jerusalem is *theology*.

Many Arabs are Islamic fundamentalists, and they believe that Muhammad is the true prophet of Allah. Their Quran is the absolute truth—it supercedes the Bible. Muhammad supercedes Christ. An infidel (a Christian or Jew) has one choice and only one in the Islamic faith—convert or be killed.

Muhammad's life can be divided into two parts—the tolerant years in Mecca and the aggressive years in Medina. The Quran reflects those two parts, and that is why at times someone will point out a teaching in the Quran that seems to indicate that Islam teaches its adherents to live at peace with their enemies. When Muhammad began to preach his revelations from Allah to the people, he believed that a peaceful religion was a good strategy for attracting people, especially the Jewish people, to the teachings of Islam.[3]

When Muhammad saw that his attempts to win over the Jews through peaceful coexistence were not successful, he "launched a new strategy, a strategy based on power. This is when he declared jihad (holy war) and went out to convert nonbelievers to Islam by the sword."[4] Muslims today are taught to interpret the Quran through a principle of progressive revelation known as *nasikh*. Any contradiction in the Quran is solved by using the newest revelation. If anyone denies the continuing revelation of Allah to Muhammad, they are denying Islam itself.[5]

We have arrived at a defining moment, when truth could conquer deception if the world would recognize that the Islamic terrorists are not *fanatics*—but *devout followers of Muhammad* who are following his example and doing what their Islamic Bible teaches them to do.

One of these devout followers of Muhammad, Indonesian jihad leader Abu Bakar Bashir, told Scott Atran of the *First Post* this chilling message: "Islam can't be ruled by others. Allah's laws must stand above human law. There is no [example] of Islam and infidels, the right and the wrong, living together in peace."[6] When asked what the West could do to make the world more peaceful, Bashir responded by saying, "They have to stop fighting Islam. That's impossible because it is *sunnatullah* [destiny, a law of nature], as Allah has said in the Koran. If they want to have peace, they have to accept to be governed by Islam."[7]

Yet, shortly after the events of 9/11, Oprah Winfrey devoted a program to what she called "Islam 101," professing it to be a crash course in the Islamic faith for her vast television audience of clueless Americans. Rod Dreher, columnist for the *New York Post*, said of that telecast: "It was grossly imbalanced and extremely dishonest. In fact, given how many Christians and other non-Muslims are horrifically persecuted today by Muslims in the name of Islam, it amounted to offensive propaganda."[8]

Dreher continued by saying:

> Oprah called Islam "the most misunderstood of the three major religions." Yet she did her best to add to the confusion by candy-coating the complicated truth about the Muslim faith. If you were to take Oprah's show as your guide to Islam, you would think Muslims were basically the Episcopalians in veils and turbans.[9]

In his 1998 book *The Clash of Civilizations and the Remaking of World Order*, Harvard University's Samuel P. Huntington warned Americans about deluding themselves concerning the true nature of the Islamic threat. "Some Westerners, including President Bill Clinton, have argued that the West does not have problems with Islam, but only with violent Islamic extremists. Fourteen hundred years of history demonstrate otherwise."[10]

We can sit around making diversity quilts and thinking happy thoughts, or we can, with charity, commit ourselves to soberly assess the historical and present-day reality of the absolute commitment of Islam to violence, to murder, and to terror toward anyone who rejects their faith.

Several years ago, Steven Emerson produced for PBS an excellent video titled *Jihad (Holy War) in America*. Its cameras went directly inside Islamic cell groups associated with mosques here in America where eager young Muslims were being recruited for holy war against the United States. Muslim leaders were shown giving speeches about bringing America to its knees through terrorism, and they made cold-blooded statements such as the following from Fayiz Azzam in Brooklyn in 1989: "Blood must flow. There must be widows, orphans...hands and limbs must be severed and limbs and blood must be spread everywhere in order that Allah's religion can stand on its feet."[11]

Is this peaceful? Does this promote brotherhood?

Many people believe today that because the world's three major religions—Judaism, Christianity, and Islam—came from the same roots, there is no reason why the three religions cannot exist side by side today in peace. But Islam follows a theology of *triumphalism*—"the dominance of one's nation, ideology, or religious creed over another." Islam teaches that Muhammad superceded the patriarchs and Christ. To a Muslim, it is Allah's will for Islam to rule the world. The word *Islam* does not mean peace—it means submission. Their objective is for everyone to be in submission to them.

That's the reason the Islamic prayer tower is the highest point in every city. It must have a position of physical supremacy. That's the reason for the impasse between Palestinian and Jew over the city of Jerusalem. Sitting in the throat of all Islamic nations is Israel—with an unconditional blood covenant from the throne of God that has given to the descendants of Abraham, Isaac, and Jacob the land of Israel *forever*. God didn't loan the land of Israel to the Jews; He gave it to them.

And that flies in the face of Islam. Islam believes the prophet Muhammad taught absolute truth—that it is God's (Allah) will for them to rule the earth. Therefore, if Islam does not defeat Israel, Muhammad and the Quran were wrong—and that's absolutely unthinkable. Therefore, they must defeat Israel. Oh, they may agree to sign a peace accord, but if they do, it will be one that is good for only seven years, and it will only be for the purpose of redeveloping their army for the destruction of Israel. If Israel survives, then Islamic theology is not true.

The real difference between the two religions, however, lies in their basis for belief. Judaism is based on the unique historical event of a divine revelation experienced by the entire nation, whereas Islam is based on the prophetic claims of a single individual who subsequently convinced others to follow his ways.[12]

Sayyid Qutb, the leading twentieth-century theoretician of Islamic fundamentalism, believed, "Humanity is standing at the brink of an abyss, not because of the threat of annihilation hanging over its head—for this is just a symptom of the disease and not the disease itself—but because humanity is bankrupt in the realm of values, those values which foster true human progress and development."[13]

While this is a symptom of modern society that nearly all Christians would agree with, they would not agree with the solution according to

Sayyid Qutb. He believes only the Quran provides for Allah's values, and he believes that Muslims can and should impose those values on the world. Any society "not dedicated to servitude to Allah alone and does not embody this servitude in its worldview and beliefs, its rituals and in its laws..." is, in Qutb's view, illegitimate. Thus any society that does not follow Islamic law as he defined it (and he wrote an eight-volume exegesis of the Quran) is according to Qutb morally perverse.[14]

In contrast to Islam, the Jewish beliefs and traditions are associated specifically with the Jewish people. Judaism strongly opposes forced conversions of other nations. The Old Testament Torah delineates the land of Israel where the Jewish people lived. Israel does not seek expansion beyond the land of Israel. Israel has withdrawn its army from territories captured after each war (for example, giving up all of the Sinai Peninsula).

The use of Islamic religion to encourage suicide bombers with the promise of heavenly life with virgins illustrates the great gap between Islam and Jewish beliefs. The Hebrew Bible prohibits killing in the Ten Commandments and completely rejects and deplores suicide. But Judaism also states, "If one comes to slay you, slay him first." This phrase is a relevant moral guide for dealing with the modern-day terrorists.[15]

The teachings of the Quran insist that no matter how mighty a nation is, it must be fought until it embraces Islam. (See Surah 9:5 earlier.) Secular America does not understand radical Islam, which is increasingly embraced with the destruction of America in mind. The growing number of extremists who take the Quran as a declaration of war against America and Israel has become a clear and present danger.

Islamic fundamentalists believe the Quran teaches them not to befriend Jews and Christians. Surah 5:51 states:

> O you who believe! take not the Jews and the Christians for your friends and protectors: they are but friends and protectors to each other. And he amongst you that turns to them (for friendship) is of them.

We have reached a theological impasse between these three religions. For a Muslim, Muhammad is the only absolute truth. It is unthinkable that he was wrong, and because Israel would not adhere to the teaching of Muhammad and convert to Islam, Israel must be defeated. Muhammad is the one who made war against Israel *holy!* If Israel survives, then Islam would be wrong, a failure, and that is an unthinkable position.

Today, jihad, or holy war, is the world's foremost source of terrorism, inspiring a worldwide campaign of violence by self-proclaimed jihadist groups, including Osama bin Laden and his Al-Qaeda network. Al-Qaeda has published a book, *The 39 Principles of Jihad,* through its Web site network that teaches terrorists how to plan and carry out the Islamic holy war of jihad. Recently exposed in a private study by Israeli researcher Colonel Jonathan D. Halevi, this book contains explicit "how-to" instructions for everything from "Performing Electronic Jihad" to "Expressing Hostility and Hatred Toward Infidels."[16]

Another terrorist agency is the Islamic Jihad, one of the most complex and dangerous of the Arab terrorist organizations. These groups generally act on their own initiative without coordination, sometimes even within the same country. All these groups share a fundamentalist Islamic ideology that espouses holy war (*jihad*) against the infidels and that is under the powerful ideological-religious influence of the Islamic revolution in Iran. The Iranian regime and the Islamic Jihad groups collaborate closely at times. Some groups not only receive aid and guidance from Iran but also enjoy generous support from other Arab and Islamic countries such as Libya, Syria, Sudan, Afghanistan, Pakistan, Saudi Arabia, and the Persian Gulf oil states. They also cooperate extensively with diverse Palestinian organizations.

The Islamic Jihad aspires to overthrow secular Arab regimes in order to establish an Islamic pan-Arab empire. Islamic Jihad is unique among the Islamic movements, however, in that it views war against the Jews and Israel ("the spearhead of the West and imperialism in the region") as an initial, essential step toward fulfilling the goals of Islam. According to the Islamic Jihad, the only way to resolve the conflict with the Jews in Palestine is by direct, violent confrontation. In 1990, one of the organization's leaders—Sheikh Tamimi (author of a 1982 booklet called *The Obliteration of Israel: A Koranic Imperative*)—expressed this principle in the following words: "The Jews have to return to the countries from which they came. We shall not accede to a Jewish state on our land, even if it is only one village."[17]

It was the Islamic revolution in Iran that triggered the growth of Islamic Jihad groups in the Arab countries. In the late 1970s, after establishing their status firmly in Iran itself, the Iranian fundamentalist revolutionaries began to "export" the Islamic revolution from their bastion to areas heavily populated by Shiites and to other Arab countries generally. The Islamic Revolutionary Council was established in Iran with this purpose in mind, and it was instructed to coordinate the activities of pro-Iranian organizations in the various countries. The Council dispatched activists to Arab countries where, with the help of local supporters and sermons delivered in the mosques, they worked to recruit young people into the Islamic Jihad. Some of the new recruits traveled to Iran to acquire a military-terrorist education, and then returned to establish additional cells in their own countries.[18]

## ISLAM AND AMERICA

Let's turn our investigation toward American Islamics. Historian Daniel Pipes, writing for *Commentary* magazine's November 2001 issue, recorded the following shocking evidence concerning Islamic's loyalty to America. "In June 1991, a convert to Islam, Siraj Wahaj, a recipient of the American Muslim community's highest honors, had the privilege of becoming the first Muslim to deliver the daily prayer in the U.S. House of Representatives. On that occasion he recited from the Quran and appealed to the almighty to guide American leaders and to 'grant them righteousness and wisdom.'"[19]

But the story about Siraj Wahaj did not end there. A little over a year later this same Muslim, addressing an audience of New Jersey Muslims, "articulated a completely different message from his mild and moderate prayer given before the U.S. House of Representatives. He said, 'If only Muslims were more clever politically, they could take over the United States and replace its constitutional government with a caliphate (Islamic leadership body).' He concluded his remarks with these words: 'If we were united and strong, we would elect our own leader and give allegiance to him....Take my word, if the six or eight million Muslims in America unite, the country will come to us.'"[20]

This is not *loyalty*—it is *sedition!* Calling for the overthrow of the

United States is resistance to or insurrection against lawful authority. In 1995 Siraj Wahaj served as a character witness for Omar Abdel Rahman at the blind Islamic terrorist's trial, which found him guilty of conspiracy to overthrow the government of the United States. More alarming still, the United States Attorney in New York listed Wahaj as one of "the unindicted persons who may be alleged as co-conspirator to blow up the twin towers in New York City in 1993."

This is the point. This Islamic leader, selected by the U.S. House of Representatives as the award-winning model of the Islamic faith in America, is on record calling for the overthrow of the United States government. Think about that when you hear a politician or talk show host on television jabbering about Islamic loyalty to America.

## ISLAM VERSUS THE TRUTH OF CHRIST

Islam and Christianity are not "sister faiths." A side-by-side examination of the texts of the Bible and of the Quran will quickly identify some of the differences related to Islam's teachings about Christ and the truths of our own Bible about the Son of God.

**1. Islam instructs its followers to kill their enemies, but Christianity instructs its followers to love their enemies.**

The Quran says to "fight and slay the Pagans wherever you find them" (Surah 9:5). But our Holy Bible tells Christ's followers to: "Love your enemies, bless them that curse you, do good to them that hate you, and pray for them which despitefully use you, and persecute you" (Matt. 5:44, KJV).

**2. Islam denies Christianity's core truth—the death and resurrection of Jesus.**

That they said (in boast), "We killed Christ Jesus the son of Mary, the Messenger of Allah";—but they did not kill him, nor crucified him, but so it was made to appear to them, and those who differ therein are full of doubts, with no (certain) knowledge, but only conjecture to follow, for of a surety they did not kill him.

—SURAH 4:157

Islam says that Jesus did not die on the cross. The Bible says that Christ died on the cross and rose from the dead.

### 3. Islam also denies the deity of Jesus Christ.

> The Jews call 'Uzair a son of Allah, and the Christians call Christ the Son of Allah....Allah's curse be on them: how they are deluded away from the Truth!
>
> —Surah 9:30

Not only does the Quran deny Christ's deity—but also, as we see in the verse from the Quran above, it also puts a curse on all who confess Jesus Christ as the Son of God. Islam brings Jesus Christ lower than Muhammad, making him no more than a messenger.

> Christ the son of Mary was no more than a Messenger; many were the Messengers that passed away before him. His mother was a woman of truth. They had both to eat their (daily) food. See how Allah makes His Signs clear to them; yet see in what ways they are deluded away from the truth!
>
> —Surah 5:75

Since there are such marked differences in these areas between Islam and Christianity, we must be prepared to test the "truth" of each. History has revealed to us that the Islamic Bible, the Quran, is a collection of the revelations Muhammad said he was given by an angel, or from a voice coming down from heaven, or sometimes as a message from a dream.[21] Christians are commanded to "try the spirits" to see if they are from God.

> Beloved, do not believe every spirit, but test the spirits, whether they are of God; because many false prophets are gone out into the world. By this you know the Spirit of God: Every spirit that confesses that Jesus Christ has come in the flesh is of God, and every spirit that does not confess that Jesus Christ has come in the flesh is not of God. And this is the spirit of the Antichrist, which you have heard was coming, and is now already in the world.
>
> —1 John 4:1–3

Every person who calls himself a prophet must be tested by Scripture. (See 1 Corinthians 14:29.)

Every revelation and every prophecy must be judged by the Word of God. If it is not scriptural—if it denies Jesus Christ as the Son of God—it is the spirit of antichrist. By applying these tests to the teachings of Muhammad, we will quickly discover that this *prophet* doesn't pass the test. From Genesis to Revelation, every page of the Bible testifies of the deity of Jesus Christ. "You shall know the truth, and the truth shall make you free" (John 8:32).

## WHO IS "ALLAH"?

The name *Allah* came from an Arabic word that had to do with the worship of the moon god in pre-Islamic Arabia. "Allah" cannot be found in the Hebrew Old Testament or the Greek New Testament.

Allah is not the same as the God of Abraham, Isaac, and Jacob. According to the Bible, God is knowable! Jesus Christ came into the world that we might know God (John 17:3). God's Word tells us that man can come into a personal relationship with God the Father. He said, "Call to Me, and I will answer you, and show you great and mighty things, which you do not know" (Jer. 33:3). God wants to love you...today...just as you are! "For God so loved the world that He gave..." (John 3:16). "God is love, and he who abides in love abides in God, and God in him" (1 John 4:16).

But in Islam, Allah is unknowable. He is so exalted that no man can ever personally know Allah. The Allah of the Quran is so distant, so far off, so abstract, that no one can know him. And Muslim believers can never *know* the love of Allah until Judgment Day when they find out if Allah loves them and will invite them into paradise. In his book *Jesus and Muhammad,* Mark Gabriel, a former devout Muslim, says: "If you ask a Muslim, 'Do you know how much Allah loves you?' he will respond, 'I don't know how much he loves me. Only Allah knows.'"[22] He gives this example from his own life:

> When I was living as a Muslim in Egypt, I was always puzzled by a little saying that the Christians used to put on their cars or frame in their shops. The phrase was *Allah Mahabe,* or *God is love.* Those two words are never put together in the Quran. I always thought, *I wonder what these people are trying to say.*[23]

The god of Islam is totally different from the God we know. The Quran tells us that the god of Islam works with Satan and demons to lead people astray in order to populate the hell he created (Surah 6:39, 126; 32:13; 43:36–37).[24]

When you turn to the Quran, you discover that Allah told Muhammad to kill and maim anyone who did not believe in Allah or in Muhammad his prophet. Jesus Christ never told His disciples to kill anyone. When Peter attacked the Roman soldier who came to arrest Christ and take Him to the cross, Jesus healed the soldier—a soldier who later nailed Him to the cross. That's love!

The love relationship between Jesus and God the Father was reflected in Jesus' relationship with His followers. Jesus told His disciples that God loved them: "The Father Himself loves you, because you have loved Me, and have believed that I came forth from God" (John 16:27).

Mark Gabriel describes the differences between our God and the god of Islam with these words: "For Jesus, God is a loving father; for Muhammad, Allah is a demanding master. This description sets the tone regarding love for all their other relationships....Allah finds new believers who will serve him better. In contrast, God the Father searches for the one lost lamb until He finds it and brings it home rejoicing. This is the difference between Allah and God."[25]

## ISLAM AND ISRAEL

Islam's attitude toward the Jews is found in Surah 9:5: "Fight and slay the Pagans [Christians and Jews] wherever you find them, and seize them, beleaguer them, and lie in wait for them in every strategem (of war)." In Surah 5:33 we read: "The punishment of those who wage war against Allah and His Messenger...is: execution, or crucifixion, or the cutting off of hands and feet from opposite sides, or exile from the land."

Muhammad taught a doctrine of triumphalism, meaning that it is God's will (Allah) for the law of Islam to rule the world. The first step in fulfilling Muhammad's dream is the destruction of Israel. No peace treaty will ever stop fourteen hundred years of Islamic hatred for the Jews. Israel cannot make peace until it has a partner who wants peace.

God's policy toward the Jewish people is found in Genesis 12:3:

I will bless those who bless you,
And I will curse him who curses you;
And in you all the families of the earth shall be blessed.

Today, the religious beliefs of Islam and Israel remain in total opposition to each other. And the front line of this religious war can be identified in the Palestinian/Israeli conflict. What is the root, the fulcrum, the cornerstone of the opposition? It is the land of Israel.

For Islam, the land of Israel is "an Islamic Waqf [Holy possession] consecrated for future Moslem generations until Judgment Day. No one can renounce it or any part, or abandon it or any part of it."[26]

In 2000, the Islamic Assembly of North America published a booklet titled *No for Normalization*, written by a Muslim scholar. He gave a similar picture of the Muslim view of land rights:

> The Jews came and attacked this land and stole it, and this will not change the fact that this land is Muslim, and it will remain that way forever. If we aren't able to liberate this land today from the Jews, this doesn't mean that we can give it up. We have to work until the time comes, and then we will bring it back to the Islamic world.[27]

This is a religious war that Islam cannot—and must not—win. It was God Himself who gave the land of Israel to Abraham, Isaac, and Jacob and their descendants forever. Israel belongs to God and to His chosen people, the Jews. And God holds the future of Israel in *His* hands, and it will be a glorious future.

# Section 2

# HOW DID WE REACH THIS POINT?

I WANT TO TAKE you on a journey through the pages of world history and sacred Scripture to personally experience Israel's past before you can grasp the magnificent future God has planned for Israel and the Jewish people.

Before you can know and understand Israel's future, you must know and understand their past. Before you can share in Israel's joy at the coming of Messiah, you must understand, to some degree, the pain and suffering of the Jewish people for the past two thousand years.

In Section 2 I want to introduce to you what Jerusalem means to God Himself. The Bible says, "I [God] have chosen Jerusalem...that My name may be there forever, and My eyes and My heart will be there perpetually...in Jerusalem, which I have chosen...I will put my name forever" (2 Chron. 6:6; 7:16; 33:7).

We will walk through ancient battle scenes as invading armies over the centuries have plundered the Holy City and taken its people captive. We will watch as a Jewish rabbi, Jesus of Nazareth, is executed. We will see the fountains of anti-Semitism begin to flow, mixing with the blood of Jewish people, through the Crusades of the Middle Ages and out of the devastation of Hitler's Holocaust.

Then we will experience the greatest prophetic miracle of the twentieth century—the rebirth of the State of Israel, May 14, 1948, at 4:32 p.m. Isaiah 66:8 (NIV) records it this way: "Can a country [nation] be born in a day?" Jerusalem was reunited under Jewish leadership for the first time in two thousand years with Israel's victory in the Six-Day War of 1967. The Bible says, "And Jerusalem will be trampled by Gentiles, until the times of the Gentiles are fulfilled" (Luke 21:24). If you listen closely, you can hear the footsteps of Messiah walking toward Israel.

# 4 JERUSALEM: THE CITY OF GOD

T HERE IS NO city on the face of the earth like Jerusalem. *Jerusalem*, the very word excites and stirs deep emotions, memories of the past, and hopes for the future.

The temple. The chanting of pilgrims. The palaces and towers. Wars and conquests. Religious longings of Jews, Muslims, and Christians. Jews praying at the Western Wall for peace in the Holy City. Jerusalem is where heaven and earth meet.

There are cities famous for their size, their industrial and manufacturing capacities, their sports teams, or their unique locations. But Jerusalem is like no city on the face of the earth.

From its earliest times, the history of Jerusalem is the history of war and peace, of greatness and misery, of splendor and squalor, of Solomon's wisdom, and of blood flowing in the gutter like rainwater in spring.

The golden thread running through that blood-soaked historical tapestry is the unshakable association of the Jewish people with the sacred city. Jerusalem is sacred to Christians, Muslims, and Jews, but God has given Jerusalem *only to the Jews*.

The Jewish love affair with Jerusalem has been interrupted through the centuries by a series of greedy and bloodthirsty conquerors, including the Egyptians, Assyrians, Babylonians, Persians, Seleucids, Romans, Muslim Arabs, Crusaders, Mamelukes, the Ottoman Empire, and the British Empire. Even today, the roots of anti-Semitism still run deep in the hearts of people throughout the world—including in our own nation. We will take a closer look at the sinful root of anti-Semitism in a later chapter and establish the need for repentance today—nationally, corporately, and individually. Anti-Semitism is sin, and sin damns the soul!

There is evidence that many Christians around the world are

beginning to own up to the role the church has played in promoting this hatred of the Jews. In an article in *Charisma* magazine in August 1996, David Aikman stated: "After centuries of intolerance, flecked with murder and crude social bigotry, increasing numbers of Christians in recent years have been owning up to the church's historical role in anti-Semitism. And they have been repenting of it."[1]

In spite of the effects of anti-Semitism expressed against them, throughout the three thousand years since David made Jerusalem the capital city, the spiritual attachment of the Jewish people to Jerusalem remains unbroken. It is a bond created by covenant between God and Abraham, which no amount of suffering or sacrifice can sever.

During the Diaspora, wherever the Jews found themselves on the face of the earth, the Jews prayed for the return to *Zion*, the biblical synonym for Jerusalem.

Their synagogues, wherever in the world they are built, were built facing Jerusalem. When the Jew built a house, part of a wall would be left unfinished, symbolizing the fact it was a temporary dwelling—until the owner could return to Jerusalem.

Without the city of Jerusalem, the State of Israel could not exist. Jerusalem is the heart and soul of Zionism. Jerusalem is now and will be in the future the center of the universe. There will be no world peace until there is peace in Jerusalem. Jerusalem is like no city on the face of the earth because Jerusalem is nothing less than the City of God.

## GOD HAS CHOSEN JERUSALEM

> I [God] have chosen Jerusalem, that My name might be there....For now I have chosen and sanctified this house [the temple], that My name may be there forever; and My eyes and My heart will be there perpetually....In this house and in Jerusalem, which I have chosen...I will put My name forever.
> —2 CHRONICLES 6:6; 7:16; 33:7

God Himself chose to establish Jerusalem as His dwelling place on earth forever. Jerusalem is the city where God's presence dwells on the earth. I have traveled around the world several times and have visited the celebrated cities of the earth, but I have found that in Jerusalem there is a very special and powerful presence. It is the literal presence of the living God of Abraham, Isaac, and Jacob. That divine presence appeared to Moses in the burning bush, calling him to liberate the Jewish people from the iron grip of Egyptian slavery.

That presence caused the crest of Mount Sinai to glow with God's glory as He gave Moses the Ten Commandments. That divine presence was on Moses' face as he descended the mount. That powerful presence can be felt at the Western Wall in Jerusalem where legions of prayers pound the gates of heaven day and night for the peace of the Jerusalem.

That presence was established by God through King David, as we can read in 1 Kings 11:36: "And to his son [Solomon] I will give one tribe, that My servant David may always have a lamp before Me in Jerusalem, the city which I have chosen for Myself, to put My name there."

The reality of that presence is validated by King David, who records the following:

> Great is the Lord, and greatly to be praised
> In the city of our God...
> Beautiful in elevation,
> The joy of the whole earth,
> Is Mount Zion...
> The city of the great King....
> God will establish it forever.
> Walk about Zion [Jerusalem],
> And go all around her.
> Count her towers;
> Mark well her bulwarks;
> Consider her palaces;
> That you may tell it to the generation following.
> For this is God,
> Our God forever and ever.
>
> —Psalm 48:1–2, 8, 12–14

> For the Lord has chosen Zion;
> He has desired it for His dwelling place.
>
> —Psalm 132:13

Jerusalem is the heart of Israel. There are voices now calling for the sacred city to be shared as a part of the Roadmap for Peace in the Middle East. Let it be known to all men far and near, the city of Jerusalem is not up for negotiation with anyone at any time for any reason in the future. It has been and shall always be the eternal and undivided capital of the State of Israel.

After the return of Israel from the Babylonian captivity, when people from other nations sought to share in the restoration of Jerusalem, Nehemiah, the Jewish governor, said to them; "The God of heaven Himself will prosper us; therefore we His servants will arise and build, but *you have no heritage or right or memorial in Jerusalem*" (Neh. 2:20, emphasis added.) It is important to see this notation—the nations of the world have no inheritance in Jerusalem.

## "IF I FORGET THEE, O JERUSALEM"

David, Israel's poet and prophet, recognized the great importance God had placed on His city, Jerusalem. For David, Jerusalem was the passion of his life, his soul. He cried out: "If I forget thee, O Jerusalem, let my right hand forget her cunning. If I do not remember thee, let my tongue cleave to the roof of my mouth; if I prefer not Jerusalem above my chief joy" (Ps. 137:5–6, KJV).

What is King David saying to us in this verse? Remember, David was a master musician who played with such skill that the demon spirits in King Saul were quieted by the melodious sounds that arose from David's heart. David was a psalmist, a songwriter, who enjoyed singing the songs of Zion.

In this verse David was saying: "If I forget Jerusalem, let me never be able to play the harp again, as my right hand will forget its cunning. If I forget Jerusalem, let me never be able to sing another song as my tongue cleaves to the roof of my mouth."

The message is very clear. If you take a master musician's ability to play his instrument away…if you take away the ability of a vocalist to sing…life has no meaning. The purpose of life is over! The passion for life and living is gone. David was saying, "If I forget Jerusalem, life has lost its meaning, its purpose, and its passion. Israel without Jerusalem would be like a human body without a heart."

## JERUSALEM, THE CITY OF PEACE

In Genesis 14:18, the Bible records that "Melchizedek king of *Salem*" blessed Abraham. *Salem* means "peaceful," and was an early name for the city of Jerusalem. *Jeru-salem* means "the city of peace."

Historically, Jerusalem has been anything but peaceful. As we look in later chapters at the history of the Jewish people, we will see that Jerusalem's citizens have been led into captivity by Nebuchadnezzar and the Babylonians. Their temples were desecrated and their citizens slaughtered by the Romans. Even today, Jerusalem is walking out the "Roadmap for Peace," a strategy to bring peace to the Middle East developed by the United States in cooperation with Russia, the European Union, and the United Nations, which was presented to Israel and the Palestinian Authority in April 2003.[2] This strategy may well prove to be a roadmap to nowhere.

Lasting peace will not come to Jerusalem until Messiah comes. He will usher in the Golden Age of Peace. At that time every man "shall beat their swords into plowshares" and study war no more (Isa. 2:4). The lion shall lie down with the lamb, and the river of life shall flow from the Temple Mount to the Dead Sea. On either side of the river of life will grow a tree of life that will bear twelve different kinds of fruit, one kind for each month. The leaves of those trees will produce healing for the nations. (See Revelation 22:1–2.)

Jerusalem is the city where Solomon built the second temple, today considered to be one of the Seven Wonders of the World. Jerusalem is the city where Jeremiah and Isaiah uttered moral and spiritual principles that shaped the standard of righteousness for the nations of the world. Jerusalem is the city where Jesus Christ, a Jewish rabbi, was crucified by the Romans as a political insurrectionist considered too dangerous to live.

Why was Jesus considered too dangerous to live by the Romans? The answer is quite simple. Any man who could feed five thousand people with the contents of a boy's sack lunch could feed an army. Anyone who could heal the injured and raise the dead could marshal legions of zealots to wage war against imperial Rome, which believed its people could not be permanently injured or killed.

Jerusalem is the city where Jesus sat on the side of the Mount of Olives and wept over Jerusalem, saying: "O Jerusalem, Jerusalem, the one who kills the prophets and stones those who are sent to her! How often I wanted to gather your children together, as a hen gathers her chicks under her wings, but you were not willing! See! Your house is left to you desolate; for I say to you, you shall see Me no more till you say, 'Blessed is He who comes in the name of the LORD" (Matt. 23:37–39).

As Christ carried His cross through the cobblestone streets of Jerusalem, He saw the women weeping for Him as He was led like a lamb to the slaughter. Jesus stopped, looked into the weeping faces of the daughters of Jerusalem, and said:

> Daughters of Jerusalem, do not weep for Me, but weep for yourselves and for your children. For indeed *the days are coming* in which they will say, "Blessed are the barren, wombs that never bore, and breasts which never nursed!"
> —LUKE 23:28–29, EMPHASIS ADDED

As Jesus looked into the future, He said, "The days are coming."

And they came. Just thirty-seven years after Jesus uttered those words, the Romans under Titus laid siege to Jerusalem. Starvation was so severe that tens of thousands of Jerusalem's inhabitants died. In a frantic effort to keep from starving to death, some of the people even resorted to cannibalism.[3]

Moses prophesied this in Deuteronomy 28:49–57 (NIV), saying:

> The LORD will bring a nation against you from far away...a fierce-looking nation without respect for the old or pity for the young. They will devour the young of your livestock and the crops of your land until you are destroyed. They will leave you no grain, new wine or oil, nor any calves of your herds or lambs of your flocks until you are ruined. They will lay siege to all the cities throughout your land until the high fortified walls in which you trust fall down. They will besiege all the cities throughout the land the LORD your God is giving you.
>
> Because of the suffering that your enemy will inflict on you during the siege, you will eat the fruit of the womb, the flesh of the sons and daughters the LORD your God has given you.... The most gentle and sensitive woman among you...will begrudge the husband she loves and her own son or daughter the afterbirth

from her womb and the children she bears. For she intends to eat them secretly during the siege and in the distress that your enemy will inflict on you in your cities.

During the siege by the Romans, Josephus relates one particular terrible incident during the siege of Jerusalem that confirms the accuracy of Moses' prophecy:

Mary, the daughter of Eleazar…a Jewish woman from a wealthy family…became so desperate with hunger that she killed her nursing infant son, roasted his flesh, and ate half of it. Attracted by the smell of roasting flesh, a group of Jewish fighters burst in on her, intending to take her food for themselves. But when the woman defiantly exposed the half-eaten body of her son and invited them to help themselves, even these hardened fighters recoiled in revulsion and left the woman to finish off her unnatural food by herself.[4]

The days of persecution and trouble for God's chosen people have continued through the centuries, as we will see in a later chapter. But God had also promised His people that He would bring them back from bondage and persecution around the world and again establish His people in Israel and restore the city of Jerusalem.

This restoration has begun. On May 14, 1948, the State of Israel was proclaimed by David Ben-Gurion. Beyond question, it was the day of greatest prophetic fulfillment during the twentieth century. It happened just as Jehovah God had declared through His prophets. Let's take a minute to review some of these prophetic declarations:

Fear not, for I have redeemed you.…
I am with you;
I will bring your descendants from the east,
And gather you from the west;
I will say to the north, "Give them up!"
And to the south, "Do not keep them back!"
Bring My sons from afar,
And My daughters from the ends of the earth.
—ISAIAH 43:1, 5–6

I will gather you from the peoples, assemble you from the countries where you have been scattered, and I will give you the land of Israel....I will give them one heart, and I will put a new spirit within them.

—Ezekiel 11:17, 19

Again I will build you, and you shall be rebuilt....
Behold, I will bring them from the north country,
And gather them from the ends of the earth,
Among them the blind and the lame,
The woman with child
And the one who labors with child, together;
A great throng shall return there.

—Jeremiah 31:4, 8

In anticipation of this great day, King David wrote:

When the Lord brought back the captivity of Zion,
We were like those who dream.
Then our mouth was filled with laughter,
And our tongue with singing.
Then they said among the nations,
"The Lord has done great things for them."

—Psalm 126:1–2

With absolute scriptural authority, it could be said that if Israel had not been brought back to the land...if the mighty right hand of God did not ransom Jacob, there would be just reason to doubt the validity of the Bible.

The regathering of the Jewish people and the rebirth of Israel is no historical aberration—the restoration of Jerusalem is a prelude to the return of the Lord. The Bible says, "When the Lord shall build up Zion [Jerusalem], he shall appear in his glory" (Ps. 102:16, kjv). Scripture makes it unmistakably clear that when the Lord returns, it will be to a sovereign Jerusalem controlled by the Jewish people.

Let me present this brief summation. In the eternal counsel of almighty God, He has determined to make Jerusalem the decisive issue by which He will deal with the nations of the earth. Those nations who align themselves with God's purposes for Jerusalem will receive His blessing. But those who follow a policy of opposition to God's purposes will receive the swift and severe judgment of God without limitation.

# 5 THE WAR AGAINST THE JEWS

ALL ROADS OF Jewish history have to lead back to Genesis 17, where God established an everlasting covenant with the father of God's chosen people, Abraham. As an old man of ninety-nine years, Abram was visited by God and given the honor of establishing a covenant with God Himself, one resulting with his descendants—God's chosen people—inheriting the land of Canaan. God did more than change Abram's name to Abraham in that visitation—He changed the course of history for all time. God told Abraham:

> As for Me, behold, My covenant is with you, and you shall be a father of many nations. . . . I will establish My covenant between Me and you and your descendants after you in their generations, for an everlasting covenant, to be God to you and your descendants after you. Also I give to you and your descendants after you the land in which you are a stranger, all the land of Canaan, as an everlasting possession; and I will be their God.
>
> —GENESIS 17:4, 7–8

But God's covenant with Abraham and His chosen people carried responsibility as well as blessing for the Jews. The point is clearly established in the Bible that *Israel's response* to the blessing of the gift of the Promised Land determined *God's response* to them. At the time of the dedication of Solomon's temple, when God's presence came down and took up residence in that holy place, God warned His people with these words:

> If you turn away and forsake My statutes and My commandments which I have set before you, and go and serve other gods, and worship them, then I will uproot them [the Jews] from My land which I have given them; and this house [temple], which I have sanctified for My name I will cast out of My sight, and will

make it a proverb and a byword among all peoples.
—2 CHRONICLES 7:19–20

It was the disobedience and rebellion of the Jews, God's chosen people, to their covenantal responsibility to serve only the one true God, Jehovah, that gave rise to the opposition and persecution that they experienced beginning in Canaan and continuing to this very day. In no way does this lessen or excuse the mistreatment and sinful atrocities the Jews have endured at the hands of their enemies, but it gives us a framework for understanding what has happened.

The words of God in the verses above were a warning. The verses that follow are no warning—they are the execution of judgment from God Himself for the disobedience of His people.

> Because they have forsaken My law which I set before them, and have not obeyed My voice, nor walked according to it, but they have walked according to the dictates of their own hearts and after the Baals...I will scatter them also among the Gentiles.
> —JEREMIAH 9:13–16

In the forty-fourth chapter of Jeremiah, God was even more specific about their acts of disobedience:

> Thus says the LORD of hosts, the God of Israel: "You have seen all the calamity that I have brought on Jerusalem and on all the cities of Judah; and behold, this day they are a desolation, and no one dwells in them, because of their wickedness which they have committed to provoke Me to anger, in that they went to burn incense and to serve other gods whom they did not know...However I have sent to you all My servants the prophets, rising early and sending them, saying, 'Oh, do not do this abominable thing that I hate!'"
> ...Then all the men who knew that their wives had burned incense to other gods, with all the women who stood by...answered Jeremiah, saying: "As for the word that you have spoken to us in the name of the LORD, we will not listen to you! But we will certainly do whatever has gone out of our own mouth, to burn incense to the queen of heaven and pour out drink offerings to her, as we have done, we and our fathers, our kings and our princes, in the cities of Judah and in the streets of Jerusalem. For

then we had plenty of food, were well-off, and saw no trouble."
—JEREMIAH 44:2–4, 15–17

How utterly repulsive, insulting, and heartbreaking to God for His chosen people to credit idols with bringing the blessings He had showered upon the chosen people. Their own rebellion had birthed the seed of anti-Semitism that would arise and bring destruction to them for centuries to come.

We are going to look briefly at some of the persecution that has faced the Jews. Some of it happened during the days in which God's Word was being written, long before the term *anti-Semitism* had been voiced by anyone. It has plagued the Jew throughout the ages. Although it rises from the judgment of God upon His rebellious chosen people, it is sin—and it damns the soul. Where it raises its ugly head today, it must be eradicated, and repentance must flow where condemnation has prevailed.

Walk with me through the centuries, and learn from the mistakes of the past. Those who fail to remember the mistakes of the past are doomed to repeat them in the future. History reveals humanity's triumphs and failures, giving us a compass for the future.

Jerusalem has been a strategic site in the Middle East for three thousand years. The sacred city has been the object of numerous attacks and sieges. Perched on easily defensible Judean hillsides less than thirty miles from the Mediterranean Sea, Jerusalem controlled the major highways that connected Egypt, Europe, and Africa. Therefore, whoever controlled Jerusalem had the ability to control the Middle East, economically and militarily. In addition to its military significance, the spiritual importance of Jerusalem to the Jews, Christians, and Muslims has made it the object of wars to gain possession of the city like no other city in the world. Those wars are not over. The greatest war the world has ever seen will soon envelop Israel and Jerusalem. The fact that it will happen, which nations will fight in that awesome battle, who will win the battle, and how many will die will be covered later in this book. But for now, let's consider some of the persecution the Jews have faced throughout the years. (I encourage you to turn to the Appendix, which contains a timeline to help you understand the history of Israel.)

## JERUSALEM AND KING DAVID

After King Saul died in shame and disgrace for consulting the witch of Endor for spiritual guidance, his dynasty continued briefly through his son Ishbosheth's reign over the northern tribes of Israel. The southern tribes, the powerful men of Judah, rallied to David, who had moved his headquarters to Hebron. For the next few years, the Israelites fought each other as much as they fought hostile enemies. The Israelites grew weary of fighting each other, and, after the violent death of Ishbosheth, they turned to David to lead them. (See 2 Samuel 5:3–8.)

At this point in history, Jerusalem was a Jebusite settlement. David attacked and drove out the Jebusites and ushered in the Golden Era of Israel. Jerusalem held the northern and southern tribes of Israel together and was the basis of economic and military control of the Middle East.

David then brought the Ark of the Covenant to Jerusalem as its permanent resting place. The ark contained the Ten Commandments and was the embodiment of the presence of Jehovah God. It had been with the Israelites throughout their forty years of wandering in the wilderness. It had carried them into battle and to victory time and again. But it had been captured by the Philistines a generation earlier. The sacred history records:

> So they brought the ark of the LORD, and set it in its place in the midst of the tabernacle that David had erected for it.
>
> —2 SAMUEL 6:17

This ark was and is the most sacred symbol Israel had because it represented the manifest presence of God. When the ark arrived in Jerusalem, the city was not only the political, economic, and military capital of the country—Jerusalem was now officially the City of God.

## JERUSALEM AND THE ASSYRIANS

But approximately two hundred years after the arrival of the ark in Jerusalem and the establishment of Jerusalem as the City of God, the Assyrians, under the leadership of King Sennacherib, conquered the northern kingdom of Israel in 722 B.C. The impact of that conquest was felt dramatically in Jerusalem by King Hezekiah. As Sennacherib and the Assyrians hammered their way south toward Jerusalem, King Hezekiah knew the battle would be won or lost over who controlled the supply of water. (See 2 Chronicles 32:1–4.)

Hezekiah knew he had to secure the source of water for Jerusalem and at the same time deny it from the enemy. No army could long endure in the searing heat of the summer without water. He solved the problem by cutting a tunnel through seventeen hundred feet of solid rock under the city from the spring of Gihon outside the city walls to the pool of Siloam within the city, so the water could run freely underground into Jerusalem.

I have been to Hezekiah's tunnel twice. My first adventure into the tunnel was one of the most exciting moments of my twenty-plus trips to Israel. With my wife, Diana, and about fifty brave friends, we followed our guide Mishi Neubach like a flock of mindless sheep into the yawning mouth of the tunnel.

However, shortly after we entered the tunnel in Jerusalem, it became very narrow and totally dark. The cool water flowing from the Gihon Spring into Jerusalem was waist high, my shoulders dragged against the sides of the tunnel, and my head atop my five-foot-eight-inch frame touched the top of the tunnel. It was an extremely tight squeeze, and some of the people with me, fighting the fear of claustrophobia, asked to go back—and did so immediately.

The rest of us pressed forward as the water rose chest high. "Does the spring ever surge and flood the tunnel?" I asked our guide Mishi Neubach, one of Israel's foremost tour guides. He assured me it did not. We pressed through the darkness until at last we saw the beautiful light of day at the other end. There is no rational reason why I repeated this adventure a second time two years later with another group. But if you are looking for a thrill when you visit the Holy Land, do it. If you are faint of heart, stay in the hotel and eat another bagel.

For those who boast of sophisticated intellects and deny that the Bible is true, what possible explanation is there for the reality of Hezekiah's tunnel? Plainly recorded in Scripture (2 Kings 20:20; 2 Chron. 32:30), the tunnel was rediscovered by archaeologists in 1880. The "Siloam Inscription," commemorating the breakthrough in the tunnel by the workers, states:

> The tunneling was completed.... While the hewers wielded the
> ax, each man toward his fellow...there was heard a man's voice
> calling to his fellow...the hewers hacked each toward the other,
> ax against ax, and the water flowed from the spring to the pool, a
> distance of 1,200 cubits. [1]

Hezekiah's tunnel is a rock that cries out to all who will hear, saying, "The Word of God is the absolute truth."

Once Hezekiah had settled the water crisis, he began to build up the broken walls of Jerusalem, raising up towers and making weapons of war for the men of Jerusalem to use in the coming battle with Sennacherib. He also made spiritual preparations for the coming war by introducing radical spiritual reforms and repairing and purifying the temple. He also broke up the idols made by the previous administration and outlawed pagan worship. He aroused the citizens of Jerusalem, saying:

> Be strong and courageous; do not be afraid nor dismayed before
> the king of Assyria, nor before all the multitude that is with
> him.... With him is an arm of flesh; but with us is the LORD our
> God, to help us and to fight our battles.
>
> —2 CHRONICLES 32:7–8

### The Assyrians attack

Sennacherib and his legions attacked the City of God in 701 B.C. Known as cold-blooded killers who tossed babies into the air and caught them on their swords, raping women and terrorizing their opponents, they surrounded the city with a sea of troops and tents as far as the eye could see. Hezekiah attempted to purchase peace by sending a letter to the king, saying, "Whatever you impose on me I will pay" (2 Kings 18:14).

Sennacherib demanded silver and gold, and Hezekiah gave him all the silver that was in his house and all that was in the Lord's house. He even stripped the gold from the doors of the temple to buy off this Assyrian terrorist. But Sennacherib only demanded more, asking Hezekiah to put two thousand men on horses so his men would have some sport as they slaughtered the Jews. This was the ultimate in ridicule.

But late at night, there was an invasion from outer space. The angel of the Lord walked through the camp of the godless cutthroat Assyrians, killing 185,000 Assyrians as they slept.

## JERUSALEM AND THE BABYLONIANS

One hundred years after God defeated the Assyrians, King Nebuchadnezzar and the Babylonians captured Jerusalem in 597 B.C. (See 2 Kings 24:8–13.) He took seven thousand Jewish captives to Babylon as craftsmen, scholars, and intellectuals to elevate the standard of living in Babylon. Daniel, Meshach, Shadrach, and Abednego were among those taken by Nebuchadnezzar in this first attack on Jerusalem, along with all the treasures of the royal palace and the temple.

Not content with his first victory over Jerusalem, in 586 B.C. Nebuchadnezzar returned to Jerusalem, causing the wholesale destruction of the city and another draft of exiles for Babylon. Jerusalem was the portrait of desolation. Its walls were torn down, its beautiful temple destroyed, homes were burnt to the ground, and most of the citizens were in exile in Babylon.

The sobs of brokenhearted Jews run deeply through the Book of Lamentations. (See Lamentations 2:5–9.) In the hearts of the exiles, Jerusalem continued to live. In the anguish of their captivity, it haunted their thoughts, and all their hopes were focused on remembering Jerusalem. In Psalm 137, the poetic pen of King David captures the mood of the exiles who were captives for seventy years.

> By the rivers of Babylon,
> There we sat down, yea we wept
> When we remembered Zion.
> We hung our harps
> Upon the willows in the midst of it.
> For there those who carried us away captive asked us a song,
> And those who plundered us requested mirth,
> Saying, "Sing us one of the songs of Zion!"
>
> How shall we sing the Lord's song
> In a foreign land?
> If I forget you, O Jerusalem,
> Let my right hand forget its skill!
> If I do not remember you,

61

Let my tongue cling to the roof of my mouth—
If I do not exalt Jerusalem
Above my chief joy.

Remember, O Lord, against the sons of Edom
The day of Jerusalem,
Who said, "Raze it, raze it,
To its very foundation!"

O daughter of Babylon, who are to be destroyed,
Happy the one who repays you as you have served us!
Happy the one who takes and dashes
Your little ones against the rock!

# 6 THE RISE OF ANTI-SEMITISM

S INCE THE REEMERGENCE of Israel on the world scene when it became
a state in 1948, subsequently regaining control of Jerusalem in 1967,
there has been a growing change of heart among Christian believers—
whether mainstream, evangelical, or charismatic—toward the Jews. In
an article in *Charisma* magazine in 1996, David Aikman stated:

> Many Christians have begun to experience a love for the Jews
> that has nothing to do with the End Times, but which is almost
> certainly the work of the Holy Spirit. It is thus important for
> all Christians...to be respectful of Jewish feelings in light of the
> uglier side of Christian history.[1]

In this chapter we are going to take a look at "the uglier side of Christian history." Although the Jewish people were persecuted and mistreated
before Jesus Christ lived and died on earth, the evil of anti-Semitism had
not gripped the world in its grasp. That evil was birthed to life as Jesus
was giving His life on a rugged cross on the lonely hill of Calvary.

We are going to explore the evil of anti-Semitism in this chapter
because it is critically important that we learn to rid ourselves of its
hold once and for all—not just for the sake of the Jews, but for our own
sakes. Unless we repent of this devastating, sinful attitude, we cannot
expect the blessing of God to flow in our lives.

When God called Abraham out of his country to a land God would
give him, God gave him a promise not only for him...not only for the
Jews, God's chosen people...but a promise that would affect every
other nation on the earth forever. God said:

> I will bless you
> And make your name great;
> And you shall be a blessing.
> I will bless those who bless you

And I will curse him who curses you;
And in you all the families of the earth shall be blessed.

—GENESIS 12:2–3

The Word could not be plainer: if you want the blessing of God upon your life, you must *bless* Israel, not *curse* it with hatred, persecution, and murder.

It is Jesus Himself who taught us to love, not hate. In Matthew 19:19, He instructs us to "…love your neighbor as yourself." As He prepared to give His life as a sacrifice for our sins, He said: "This is My *command-ment*, that you love one another as I have loved you…You are my friends if you do whatever I command you" (John 15:12, 14, emphasis added). He was even more direct in Matthew 5:44–45, where He instructed:

> But I say to you, love your enemies, bless those who curse you, do good to those who hate you, and pray for those who spitefully use you and persecute you, that you may be sons of your Father in heaven.

Hatred is simply not an option for people who want to serve God and have His blessing upon their lives. Yet it was the crucifixion of the Son of God that has given rise to the hatred and persecution of God's own people.

For centuries, the Jews have been beaten, murdered, robbed, and raped while fanatics have screamed, "You are the Christ killers!" This vicious label has been tied about the necks of the Jewish people since shortly after the death of Christ, causing Europe and the Middle East to turn red with Jewish blood.

Let's take a closer look at what has occasioned such venomous hatred to be expressed toward God's chosen people. Perhaps the one question that has caused such virulent hatred to be loosed is this: *Who killed Jesus?*

## EYEWITNESS ACCOUNTS OF THE CRUCIFIXION

The Book of Matthew gives us two important facts about the death of Christ:

- There was a crucifixion plot.

- The plot was carried out by the high priest Caiaphas,

political appointee of Rome by Herod the Great, who
had conquered Rome before the birth of Christ. (See
Matthew 26:3.)

As a people, the Jews had nothing to do with the political conspiracy against Jesus Christ. The high priest Caiaphas was appointed by Herod to do the will of Rome. He was an illegitimate priest who was not selected by the Jewish people to do their will.

Into this political setting came a Jewish rabbi named Jesus of Nazareth. The Jews were looking for a deliverer who would lead a revolt to break the oppressive chains of Rome. The popularity of Jesus spread like chained lightning. Anyone who could heal and raise people from the dead could heal wounded soldiers and raise dead troops back to life to fight the pagan Romans.

Jesus was a very serious political threat to Herod and his stooge high priest Caiaphas. So they entered into a politically inspired plot to have Jesus of Nazareth killed Roman style…the crucifixion!

The high priest and his circle of religious conspirators had no mandate from the Jewish people; rather, "they feared the people." They most certainly did not represent the one million Jews that were living in Israel at the time, much less all the Jews that lived in Egypt or were scattered over the Roman Empire. These religious rogues were a miniscule handful led by the high priests to do Rome's bidding.

In the Gospel of Luke, Jesus Himself identifies His killers: "Then He took the twelve aside and said to them, 'Behold, we are going up to Jerusalem, and all things that are written by the prophets concerning the Son of Man will be accomplished. For He will be *delivered to the Gentiles* [the Romans] and will be mocked and insulted and spit upon. They will scourge Him and kill Him. And the third day He will rise again" (Luke 18:31–33, emphasis added).

The Bible text is perfectly clear. Jesus was crucified by Rome as a political insurrectionist considered too dangerous to live. He was a threat to Herod's grip on Palestine. He was a threat to the high priest. The Calvary plot among Herod's inner circle produced the Roman crucifixion of Jesus of Nazareth. It had nothing to do with the will of the Jewish people as a civilization.

The historical fact is that three out of four Jews did not live in Israel when Jesus began His ministry. Nine out of ten of the Jews in Israel during His ministry lived outside of Jerusalem.[2]

The justice of God would never permit judgment for the sins of a handful of people to be passed to a civilization of people. In the last breath of His earthly life, Jesus forgave even the high priest and his conspirators: "Father, forgive them, for they do not know what they do" (Luke 23:34.)

If God has forgiven...why can't Christianity?

## JUST HOW JEWISH WAS JESUS?

It is essential for all anti-Semites to separate Jesus from His Jewish roots. Why? If you can separate Jesus from the Jewish people, hatred becomes fashionable, and anti-Semitism becomes a Christian virtue. An anti-Semite is a dead Christian whose hatred has strangled his faith. Like a chameleon, anti-Semitism can masquerade alternately as *doing the will of God* or *political ideology.*

If Jesus can be separated from His Jewish roots, Christians can continue to praise the dead Jews of the past (Abraham, Isaac, and Jacob) while hating the Goldbergs across the street. But when you see the Jewish people as the family of our Lord, they become our extended family whom we are commanded to love unconditionally.

Most Christians think of Jesus and His twelve disciples as Christians before their time. Not so! Jesus was not a Christian. He was born to Jewish parents. He was dedicated in the Jewish tradition, reared studying the words of Moses and the prophets of Israel, and became a Jewish rabbi. He died with a sign over his head on which was written in three languages, "This is the King of the Jews."

It was Jesus of Nazareth, this Jewish rabbi, who, with the following words, instructed His twelve Jewish disciples to take the light of the gospel to the Gentile world:

> Go into all the world and preach the gospel to every creature.
> —MARK 16:15

Before His death, Jesus agonized in prayer to His Father, God, asking God to protect and guide His disciples as they stepped into the world with the message of peace and salvation. He prayed for the unity of all who would believe in Him with these words:

> As You sent Me into the world, I also have sent them into the
> world....I do not pray for these alone, but also for those who
> will believe in Me through their word; that they all may be one,
> as You, Father, are in Me, and I in You; that they also may be one
> in Us, that the world may believe that You sent Me.
>
> —JOHN 17:18, 20–21

But the evil of hatred for God's people, the Jews, has hindered this
prayer from God's own Son from being fulfilled.

The first-century Gentiles and Jews who followed Christ met
together in unity. They sang the same songs. They kept the same festi-
vals. They had the same rabbi—Jesus of Nazareth.

Then came the crucifixion. Jesus of Nazareth ascended into heaven in
the sight of the twelve apostles, and the church of Jesus Christ was left
alone. One of the first church problems was what to do with the Gentile believers who were worshiping with the Jewish believers. Should the
Gentiles be circumcised? Should the Gentiles keep the Law of Moses?
How strict were the Jews going to be with the new Gentile believers who
had just come out of absolute paganism to follow Jesus of Nazareth?

This is when the Jerusalem Council, as recorded in Acts 15, occurred.
James, the brother of Jesus Christ, stated that the Gentile followers of
Christ had to follow some strict guidelines in order to continue worshiping with their Jewish fellow believers. It would not be necessary for them
to be circumcised, but they must stop committing fornication, and they
must stop eating meats that were offered to idols. (See Acts 15:24–29.)

For a while, the Jews and Gentile Christians continued to worship
together in harmony. Then came the Romans under the leadership
of Titus, bringing death and famine like none could have possibly
imagined.

## THE SIEGE OF JERUSALEM

The siege of Jerusalem by Titus began in April, A.D. 70, during the
Passover. The armies of Romans surrounded the city of Jerusalem,
trapping tens of thousands of Jews behind the walls of the sacred city.
The Romans closed all exits from Jerusalem, even the tunnels under
the wall, and the siege continued for months. All hope for escape was

lost, and a horrible famine resulted for those remaining in the city. The horrors of the famine in the city of Jerusalem during the siege of Titus reached far beyond the imagination of mortals to comprehend. All human emotions yield to hunger, thus it was reported by Josephus:

> Wives snatched food from their husbands, children from their fathers, and, most pitiful of all, mothers snatched food out of the very mouths of their infants; while their dearest ones were dying in their arms, they did not hesitate to deprive them of the life-giving morsels.[3]

After months of the siege, the brutal power of the Roman army crushed Jerusalem. Titus and the Roman army set the gates of the temple on fire and ordered the complete destruction of the city of Jerusalem, even to the tearing down of the walls so that not one stone was left on top of the other. Jesus had prophesied this event in Matthew 24:2, when He said, "Do you not see all these things? Assuredly, I say to you, not one stone shall be left here upon another, that shall not be thrown down." It literally came to pass when Titus destroyed Jerusalem.

Josephus records, "...the number of those that were carried captive during this whole war was collected to be ninety-seven thousand as was the number of those that perished during the whole siege, eleven-hundred thousand."[4]

Eleven hundred thousand equals 1.1 million people dead at the hands of the Romans, mostly through brutal starvation.

Most of the ninety-seven thousand prisoners were taken to Rome where they were fed to lions to amuse the bloodthirsty Roman citizens in the Roman coliseum, or forced to become gladiators and fight to the death. Some, who were believed to be criminals, were burned alive.

## GENTILE CHRISTIANS SEPARATE FROM JEWS

Before Titus instructed the Roman army to close the gates and stop any people from escaping from the city of Jerusalem, he had made it known to those behind the walls that anyone desiring to leave the city could do so without harm prior to the commencement of battle. The Hellenistic Christians of Greek influence, who resided in the city, had no loyalty to the city of Jerusalem. With tens of thousands of people lying dead in the streets from starvation and thousands more thrown over the walls, causing a putrid smell to cover the city, the Hellenistic Christians accepted Titus's invitation to leave Jerusalem and went to a town in Transjordan called Pella. Thus this terrible invasion from Titus had brought about the separation of Gentiles and Jews who were followers of Jesus Christ, and that separation has remained until this day. With that separation, the seeds of anti-Semitism—begun centuries before when the Jews began to be persecuted by the former inhabitants of the Promised Land, and watered by the controversy of who was responsible for the death of Christ—broke ground and began to bear its ugly fruit of violence.

## THE JEWISH FORTRESS OF MASADA

After the fall of Jerusalem in A.D. 70, Masada was the last flickering flame of freedom for the Jewish people. Masada is located twenty miles south of Sdom on the Dead Sea and rises thirteen hundred feet into the sky with a flat top of one-half mile.

Built by Herod the Great in 40 B.C. as a fortress, after the fall of Jerusalem at the hands of Titus it was occupied by a small group of Jewish patriots who escaped from Jerusalem under the leadership of Eleazar. He was the nephew of Menahem, who had earlier defeated the Romans who occupied it, thus putting it back in Jewish hands. For nearly three years, Eleazar and the Jewish patriots held out against the Roman legion that had encircled the mountain, trying in vain to storm the mountain fortress.

By A.D. 73, the Roman army under the leadership of Hadrian had grown to ten thousand men, bivouacked in eight camps in the valley. The Romans started to build an assault ramp to the top, using thousands of slaves, many of whom were Jewish. After nine months the ramp was complete, and the Romans succeeded in moving a battering ram against the wall. They broke through the stone wall, but the defenders had managed to build a wall of earth and wood that was flexible and hard to break. Eventually, the Romans managed to destroy it by fire and decided to enter the fortress the next day.

That night Eleazar gathered all the defenders, giving an impassioned plea that they should all commit suicide by their own hand rather than allow the Romans to rape their wives and daughters and place their sons in chains of eternal slavery. When the Romans came in full battle dress the next morning, they were met by the thunderous sound of silence. They discovered that nearly all of the 960 Jews who had held out for three years had committed suicide. Two women and five children, who had hidden in a cave, came out and informed the Romans of this daring act of freedom. It is a moment in Jewish history that will be remembered for eternity.

I have taken thousands of pilgrims to Masada to fully understand Israel's past and present. The access to Masada from the east is by a road going from Sdom to Jericho along the edge of the Dead Sea, the lowest elevation on Planet Earth. Many believe the sulfuric odor of the Dead Sea and its low elevation bear witness to the fact this was probably the place where God blasted Sodom and Gomorrah with hailstones. The city was so totally demolished that archaeologists have never been able to find Sodom and Gomorrah to this day.

When the road turns toward Masada, it rises hundreds of feet up out of the Judean Desert and can be seen for miles. You can travel to the top of Masada either by walking up the ancient, aptly named "Snake Path" or by taking a cable car to the top. I highly recommend that you take the cable car.

In the twentieth century, Masada became a symbol of courage for the emerging Jewish state. In 1949, at the end of the War of Independence, the Israeli flag was hoisted on Masada's summit as a symbol for the Jewish people that they would now be free from any form of tyranny or terrorism.

Yet, as Iran prepares nuclear weapons, there are few doubts those weapons may be used on Israel first. But Israel is not obligated to commit national suicide for world peace. Israel has the right of every democracy to defend itself against tyranny and terrorism! They did so at Masada…and they will do so in the future.

When you go to Israel—don't miss Masada!

# 7 CENTURIES OF MISTREATMENT

THREE HUNDRED YEARS following Christ's crucifixion in Jerusalem and the slaughter of the Jews by the Romans under the leadership of Titus and Hadrian, the Hellenistic Christians who had fled from Jerusalem and taken up residence in Transjordan were being influenced by the Greeks to blame—not Rome—but the Jewish people for the death of Christ.

How did the Gentile and Jewish followers of Christ become separated? How did a Jewish rabbi named Jesus Christ of Nazareth and twelve disciples begin an organization that three hundred years later adopted a policy to kill Jews? A brief and greatly oversimplified explanation is as follows.

When Jesus of Nazareth was crucified in A.D. 33, the New Testament church consisted of mostly Jews and some Gentile believers. They were not yet called Christians but were referred to as "God-fearers."

The first source of contention in the New Testament Church was doctrinal division as recorded in Acts 15. The Jewish believers wanted to know if the Gentiles had to be circumcised in order to be saved. James, the brother of Jesus and the pastor of the Jerusalem Church, stood and delivered a powerful message declaring that Gentiles did not need to be circumcised. Thank God for Pastor James. James stated that Gentiles must abstain from immorality and meats offered to idols.

Thirty-seven years after the crucifixion in A.D. 70, the Roman army of eighty thousand hardened combat veterans under Titus besieged the city of Jerusalem. No one in . . . no one out. According to Josephus, approximately 1.1 million Jews died in this siege.

Many Gentile believers fled the city and went to Pella, a city sixty miles northeast of Jerusalem. The physical separation of Gentile and Jewish followers of Christ had begun and would never be restored. The Jews saw the Gentiles' leaving as an act of betrayal.

The permanent separation of Jews and Gentiles occurred in one day with one historic document when Constantine signed the Edict of Toleration, also known as the Edict of Milan, in A.D. 313, officially recognizing *Christianity* as the state religion. The Roman Church grew in power until it ruled most of the known world through Papal States.

When the early Jewish Christians began preaching the gospel to the Gentiles, they still clung to their Jewish roots and faith. But by the second century A.D., the evolving doctrine of replacement theology had begun to permeate the thinking of the early church. Replacement theology teaches that the church has completely replaced national Israel in God's plan. Adherents of replacement theology believe that the Jews are no longer God's chosen people, and God does not have specific future plans for the nation of Israel.[1]

In his book *The Crucifixion of the Jews*, Franklin Littell states:

> The cornerstone of Christian anti-Semitism is the superseding or displacement myth, which already rings with the genocidal note. This is the myth that the mission of the Jewish people was finished with the coming of Jesus Christ, that "the old Israel" was written off with the appearance of "the new Israel." To teach that a people's mission in God's providence is finished, that they have been relegated to the limbo of history, has murderous implication which murderers will in time spell out.[2]

## An Overview of Hatred

Anti-Semitism in Christianity began with the statements of the early church fathers, including Eusebius, Cyril, Chrysostom, Augustine, Origen, Justin, and Jerome. These men published papers and historical pamphlets, some of which are included in what is known as *Adversus Judaeos*.

This poisonous stream of venom came from the mouths of spiritual leaders to virtually illiterate congregants, sitting benignly in their pews, listening to their pastors. They labeled the Jews as "the Christ killers, plague carriers, demons, children of the devil, bloodthirsty pagans who look for an innocent child during the Easter week to drink his blood, money hungry Shylocks, who are as deceitful as Judas was relentless."[3]

John Chrysostom (A.D. 345–407), who was called the "Bishop with the Golden Mouth," was the first to use the term "Christ killers." It was a vicious label the Jews were never able to escape. Recorded in his homilies is this description of the Jews:

> The Jews are the most worthless of all men. They are lecherous, greedy and rapacious. They are perfidious *murderers of Christ*. They worshiped the devil; their religion is a sickness. The Jews are the odious assassins of Christ, and for killing God there is no expiation possible, no indulgence or pardon. Christians may never cease vengeance, and the Jews must live in servitude forever. God always hated the Jews. It is incumbent upon all Christians [their duty] to hate the Jews.[4]

## JERUSALEM'S WAR WITH THE CRUSADERS

The Roman Catholic Church, which was supposed to carry the light of the gospel, plunged the world into the Dark Ages. The Crusaders are often presented as holy men on the road from Europe to Jerusalem and back pursuing a righteous cause with the blessing of the pope. Nothing could be further from the truth.

The Crusaders were a motley mob of thieves, rapists, robbers, and murderers whose sins had been forgiven by the pope in advance of the Crusade. Any holy warrior who answered the pope's call of the crusade could consider all his financial debts to any Jewish creditor canceled, which reduced many Jewish communities to poverty.[5] For a man looking for adventure, it was an instant way to become debt free.

What caused the Crusades?

Historians dance around this simple question with a myriad of wordy responses that avoid and evade historical reality. The brutal truth is that the Crusades were military campaigns of the Roman Catholic Church to gain control of Jerusalem from the Muslims and to punish the Jews as the alleged Christ killers on the road to and from Jerusalem.

In 1095, Pope Urban II preached (the call for Crusade) at Clare-mont, appealing to the French to recover the Holy Land for Christianity. The response was immediate and positive.

The Crusaders were all too conscious, however, of the great distance between Europe and Jerusalem. Therefore, before attacking Muslims...and the Jews of Jerusalem...they first moved against the

Jews of Europe. "Kill a Jew and save your soul" became the battle cry of the Crusaders.[6]

When the first Crusade under Godfrey reached Jerusalem in 1099, the Crusaders invaded the city through the Jewish quarter. In a desperate attempt to save their lives, Jewish men, women, and children ran to the synagogue for protection, locking the doors behind them.

The Crusaders promptly set fire to the synagogue and listened to helpless women and innocent children scream in horror, begging for mercy as they were burned alive. The Crusaders marched around the synagogue singing triumphantly "Christ We Adore Thee" as 969 members of the family of our Lord were cremated.[7]

Jerusalem was captured by the Crusaders on July 15, 1099, with most of the Jewish population, which numbered between twenty and thirty thousand, slaughtered that very day. The Jews who were not burned alive in the synagogue as the Crusaders marched around it were sold into slavery in Italy.[8]

## Blood libel

During the Dark Ages, the Jews sought to survive in an increasingly hostile and threatening Christian world. The Dutch humanist Erasmus captured the prevailing mood of the era saying, "If it is the part of a good Christian to detest the Jews, then we are all good Christians."[9]

It was during this era that Christians fabricated the preposterous story that Jews were kidnapping innocent Christian children, ritually slaughtering them, and using their blood in making unleavened bread for Passover.

The first recorded blood libel occurred in Norwich, England, in A.D. 1144. A boy named William had disappeared, and Christians sent out an alarm. Theobald of Cambridge, an apostate Jew, approached the authorities and charged the Jews with having murdered the boy. (History records that the Jews have been persecuted most by fellow Jews.) Theobald told the authorities that the Jews had been following an ancient custom of sacrificing a Christian child during the Passover festival and that representatives of Jews throughout the world had assembled in Narbonne, France, to decide who would carry out the murder.

According to his story, the assembly at Narbonne had cast lots, and the honor of carrying out the ritual murder had fallen on the Jews of Norwich. When the boy's body was found in Norwich, however, it showed no evidence of murder. Therefore, no one was punished. Nevertheless, the boy, William of Norwich, was declared a martyr, and a memorial chapel and shrine were erected in his honor in Norwich.

By the thirteenth century, several leaders of the church, as well as Emperor Frederick II, attempted to refute and forbid the blood libel. In 1245, Pope Innocent IV issued a papal bull forbidding blood libel, which, he said, was groundless. He declared it was a mockery of Christ's teachings that led only to evil.

Pope Gregory X banned the accusation in another bull in 1274. Others popes also denounced it. Unfortunately, their decrees were ineffective since the blood libel was an easy way for anti-Semitic demagogues to manipulate mobs. By the seventeenth century, ritual murder accusations had spread to Eastern Europe and Russia, where they continued until the early years of this century.[10]

## THE SPANISH INQUISITION (A.D. 1478–1808)

The Spanish Inquisition was perhaps the most cynical plot in the black history of Catholicism, aimed at expropriating the property of wealthy Jews and converts in Spain for the benefit of the royal court and the Roman Catholic Church. Even dead Jews were dug up and put on "trial" so their estates could be confiscated from their heirs.[11]

When Tomas Torquemada was appointed by the church as Inquisitor General of Spain in 1483, he printed *Manuals of Inquisition*, which told the citizens of Spain how to spot a Jew or a *maranno* (pig), a term used to identify those who converted to Judaism. Once caught, these people were to be brought to trial by the Roman Catholic Church.

The *trial* was actually a torture chamber using fire, garrote, rack, whip, and needle to force those on trial to confess their sin of converting to Judaism, or of being "closet" Jews. Inquisitional tortures continued well into the eighteenth century. During that time, 323,362 people were burned, and 17,659 were burned in effigy. It is one of the darkest periods in Spanish history.[12]

## PERSECUTION IN EUROPE

Throughout Europe, during the Crusades and the Dark Ages, and for several following centuries, very few Jewish households escaped without being robbed, tortured, or murdered. The following list highlights some of the anti-Semitic violence carried out during this time.

- *London, England*—Four hundred Jews were massacred on Palm Sunday (1263). Six hundred eighty Jews were imprisoned in the tower, and 290 were hanged (1290). In A.D. 1290, an expulsion order was given for all Jews to leave England by November 1. This was the first general expulsion of Jews from any country in the Medieval Period.[13]

- *Edward I, England*—Edward I drove 16,500 Jews from England, and for four hundred years, until Cromwell granted permission for them to return, England was free of the Jewish people.

- *France*—France drove 100,000 Jewish people out of France in 1306, and the crown confiscated their possessions. After ten years, however, they were recalled when the kingdom felt need of their commercial abilities.

- *Germany*—At the time of the Black Death (1348–1350), Jewish people were accused of poisoning wells and springs of the Christians. They were subject to fearful tortures, and innocent people were forced into confessions. One quarter of the population died of the plague, and the Jewish people were blamed.

- *Strasburg, Germany*—In Strasburg, 2,000 victims were burned on a gigantic scaffold. Whole communities throughout Germany were destroyed. Many Jewish people burned their homes and perished in the flames rather than wait to die at the hands of those who carried a cross and professed to serve the loving Christ.

# Martin Luther
## (A.D. 1483–1546)

It was Martin Luther whose anti-Semitism was deeply appreciated by Adolf Hitler. "The worst, evil genius of Germany," wrote Dean Inge, "is not Hitler, or Bismarck, or Frederick the Great, but Martin Luther."[14]

When Martin Luther introduced the Reformation, he was convinced that the Jewish people would be delighted with his new version of Christianity and would join him in an assault on the Roman Catholic Church. He was wrong! In the beginning, Luther made complimentary remarks about the Jewish contribution to Christianity. When the Jews did not follow him, he turned on them with a vulgarity and a vengeance that greatly appealed to the German people.

His doctrine provided many suitable texts for Hitler's program of extermination. The most vicious, Jew-hating statements Luther ever made were to be found in his tract entitled "Concerning the Jews and Their Lies." In it he stated:

> Let me give you my honest advice.
>
> First, their synagogues or churches should be set on fire. And whatever does not burn up should be covered or spread over with dirt so that no one may ever be able to see a cinder or stone of it. And this ought to be done for the honor of God and of Christianity in order that God may see that we are Christians....
>
> Secondly, their homes should be broken down and destroyed. Thirdly, they should be deprived of their prayer books and the Talmud in which such idolatry, lies, cursing, and blaspheme are taught. Fourthly, their rabbis must be forbidden under the threat of death to teach anymore....
>
> Fifthly, passport and traveling privileges should be absolutely forbidden to Jews. Let them stay at home. Sixthly, they ought to be stopped for usury. For this reason, as said before, everything they possess they stole and robbed us through their usury, for they have no other means of support. Seventhly, let the young and strong Jews and Jewesses be given the flail, the axe, the hoe, the spade, the distaff, and spindle, and let them earn their bread by the sweat of their noses as is enjoined upon Adam's children.

We ought to drive the lazy bones out of our system.

If, however, we are afraid that they might harm us personally, or our wives, children, servants, cattle, et cetera...then let us apply the same cleverness (expulsion) as the other nations, such as France, Spain, Bohemia, et cetera...and settle with them for that which they have extorted from us, and after having it divided up fairly, let us drive them out of the country for all time.

To sum up, dear princes and notables who have Jews in your domains, if this advice of mine does not suit you, then find a better one so that you and we may all be free from this inseparable Jewish burden...the Jews.[15]

A couple of years after writing this tract, Martin Luther died!

## NAZI ANTI-SEMITISM

The Bible says, "Whatever a man sows, that he will also reap" (Gal. 6:7). The law of seedtime and harvest begins at the gates of Genesis and never ends. If you sow love, you reap love. If you sow hate, you reap hate. After hundreds of years of Jewish hatred pouring out toward the Jews, the harvest of hate was reaped in a nightmare known as *the Holocaust.*

Adolf Hitler loved Luther's theology. His Nazi machine showed "a proper appreciation of the continuity of their history when they declared that the first large-scale Nazi pogrom (violent persecution of the Jews), in November 1938, was a pious operation performed in honor of the anniversary of Martin Luther's birthday."[16]

Adolf Hitler is perceived by the Jewish people of the twenty-first century as just another crusader who walked across the stage of history, systematically slaughtering six million Jews, claiming that it was "the will of God."

It doesn't require a great intellect to deduct that if our Jewish friends believed Hitler was a Christian in good standing, our generation must expose him for who he truly was, denounce him, and conduct ourselves according to the law of Jesus Christ who said, "Love your neighbor as yourself" and "Do unto others as you would have them do unto you."

Anti-Semitism is sin, and as sin it damns the soul. Most readers will be shocked by the clear record of history linking Adolf Hitler and the Roman Catholic Church in a conspiracy to exterminate the Jews.

In his book *Mein Kampf* [My Struggle], Hitler raved, saying, "Hence today, I believe that I am acting in accordance with the will of the Almighty Creator: by defending myself against the Jew, I am fighting for the work of the Lord."[17]

One of the largest extermination pits, at Kerch, was examined in 1942 by officials in the Russian army. This was their report:

> It was discovered that this trench—1 kilometer in length, 4 meters in width, and 2 meters in depth—was filled to overflowing with bodies of women, children, old men, and boys and girls in their teens. Near the trench were frozen pools of blood. Children's caps, toys, ribbons, torn-off buttons, gloves, milk bottles, and rubber comforters, small shoes, galoshes, together with torn-off hands and feet, and other parts of human bodies were lying nearby. Everything was spattered with blood and brains.[18]

How could this madness happen at the hands of one of the most civilized and cultured nations on the face of the earth? How could it be justified in the minds of the Christian-baptized German people? It was done with the oft-repeated poisonous phrase: "The Jews are the Christ killers."

Dr. James Parks writes: "In our day...more than six million deliberate murders are the consequences of the teachings about Jews for which the Christian church is ultimately responsible...which has its ultimate resting place in the teaching of the New Testament itself."[19] One of those deadly New Testament myths is that the Jews killed Jesus. No justification can be found in the New Testament to support that myth.

## HITLER AND THE CATHOLIC CHURCH

Adolf Hitler attended a Catholic school as a child and heard all the fiery anti-Semitic rantings from Chrysostom to Martin Luther. When Hitler became a global demonic monster, the Catholic Church and Pope Pius XII never, ever slightly criticized him.

Pope Pius XII, called by historians "Hitler's Pope," joined Hitler in the infamous Concordat of Collaboration, which turned the youth of the Germany over to Nazism, and the churches became the stage background for the bloodthirsty cry, *"Pereat Judea."*[20]

Those who do not remember the mistakes of the past are destined to repeat them in the future. Let all ministers of the gospel of Jesus Christ in the twenty-first century unite to stand against every form of anti-Semitism, lest we deserve the scathing words of the prophet Isaiah, "They are all dumb dogs, they cannot bark…," in the day of danger (Isa. 56:10). A dumb dog is one that refuses to bark when danger approaches; therefore, it is worthless. America's pulpits are full of them. They preach, not from a burning passion, but as a paid profession.

Nazi *legality* was immensely strengthened by the concordat with the Vatican (July 20, 1933), an agreement that the Catholic Church had refused to grant the previous Weimar Republic. Hitler described the Concordat of Collaboration as an "unrestricted acceptance of national socialism by the Vatican." Indeed it was, since it subordinated all of cultural and educational activities of the church to Nazi ideology and regimen. It began with the placing of Hitler's portrait on the walls of all Catholic, parochial, and Sunday schools, and ended with the church bells ringing at every Nazi victory, including the arrest and transportation of the last Jew from every town and hamlet in Germany.[21]

The sell-out of Catholicism to Hitler began not with the people but with the Vatican itself. For Rome, it was only a repetition of the concordat it had previously made with Mussolini. The German bishops followed the Vatican, represented by the Secretary of State, Cardinal Pacelli, and later Pope Pius XII. The priests obeyed the bishops, and the parishioners fell in line.

Not once after the signing of the concordat did the Roman Catholic Church protest against Hitler or his barbarianism, including the shedding of blood of a million Jewish children. When protests came, they were invariably concerned with infractions against the interest of the church. On Hitler's fiftieth birthday, April 20, 1939, Protestant and Catholic bishops of all but two dioceses in Germany urged the following prayer in pastoral letters to the faithful: "Remember, O Lord, our Fuhrer, whose secret wishes thou knowest. Protect him with thy inexhaustible kindness. Give him the victory of Heaven for him and his foe."[22]

Was Hitler a Christian? The Roman Catholic Church certainly thought so. In all of his years of absolute brutality, he was never denounced or even scolded by Pope Pius XII or any Catholic leader in the world. To those Christians who believe that Jewish hearts will be warmed by the sight of the cross, please be informed—to them it's an electric chair. It is the symbol of death under which their relatives, for two thousand years, have been brutally massacred by those who claimed to be serving the loving Christ.

## THE CATHOLIC CHURCH RECONCILES WITH THE JEWS

Most of the world will remember Pope John Paul II as the second longest serving pope in history, the most traveled, and the most seen. He will be remembered for staring down Communism and embracing people of all faiths and colors. He will be lovingly remembered for his bold stand against abortion.

But for the Jewish people, the apple of God's eye, the most crucial elements of John Paul II's work was reconciling the Roman Catholic Church with its anti-Semitic past, memorializing the Holocaust, and officially recognizing the State of Israel. As Pope John Paul II began to prepare the Roman Catholic Church for the Jubilee 2000 celebrations, he proclaimed the first Sunday in Lent, March 12, to be the "Day of Pardon." "On that day the whole Church was called to a collective act of repentance for the historical sins of the Church's sons and daughters....Seven representatives of the Church...step forward to offer prayers for sins committed in the service of the truth, such as during the Crusades and the Inquisition....After each cardinal and bishop offers a prayerful petition, John Paul replies with his own."[23]

Some have said he will be remembered as "the best pope the Jews ever had."[24]

Rabbi David Rosen, the director of the American Jewish Committee's Interreligious Affairs Department, said, "No pope has devoted himself as much to advancing positive relations between the Christian world and the Jewish people as this pope. He may indeed be described as a hero of reconciliation."[25]

In his brief reign as pope, it appears as if Pope Benedict XVI will faithfully continue the righteous works of Pope John Paul II. In his first major interfaith meeting, Pope Benedict XVI assured a delegation of Jewish leaders of the Roman Catholic Church's commitment to fighting anti-Semitism and to closer ties between Jews and Catholics.

> My predecessor, Pope Paul VI and, in a particular way, Pope John Paul II, took significant steps toward improving relations with the Jewish people. It is my intention to continue on this path.[26]

In 1983 in Houston, Texas, I spoke to a packed house at the Music Hall, conducting an event I'd founded years earlier known as "A Night to Honor Israel." In the speech attacking anti-Semitism as sin, and as sin it damns the soul, I called upon Christians of America to repent of any and every form of anti-Semitism. The next morning the *Houston Chronicle* carried that call to repentance as its headline story. I was stunned that a simple call for Christians to do what Christ taught, to "love your neighbor as yourself," would even be considered worthy of a headline story in one of America's foremost cities.

It's time for all Christians to stop praising the dead Jews of the past, Abraham, Isaac, and Jacob, while resenting the Jews across the street. They are our brothers and sisters who worship the God of Abraham, Isaac, and Jacob just as we do.

Remember that all anti-Semitism will come into judgment at the Judgment of the Nations. The basis of this judgment will be how individuals and nations treated Israel and the Jewish people.

# 8

## JERUSALEM REGAINS INDEPENDENCE

THE JEWS OF Palestine lived under the confines of the Balfour Declaration and what became known as the *British Mandate* (the Palestine Mandate of the League of Nations) from 1917 until 1948.

The Balfour Declaration, a letter to Lord Rothschild by British Foreign Secretary Arthur James Balfour, written November 2, 1917, became the "basis movement to create a Jewish state in Palestine."[1] The British Mandate, introduced July 24, 1922, was far more partial to the Arabs living in Palestine than it was to Jewish people. In truth, the British Mandate wanted to give the Jewish people a home without giving them the right of self-determination while living in the Promised Land of their fathers.[2]

The escalating conflict between the Arabs and Jews in Palestine and the devastating rise of Hitler's Holocaust in Europe caused many Jews to try to flee for safety. Hitler was killing up to twenty thousand Jews per day in the Nazi death camps, and the terrified Jews came scrambling to Palestine, some in decrepit ships by sea, and others walking long miles through Europe after selling every possession they had to reach the Promised Land. Others attempted to flee to Britain or other Allied countries.

Many never made it to safety. In his captivating book *The Revolt*, former Israeli Prime Minister Menachem Begin described how the British army captured Jews during the time of the British Mandate and sent them to Europe, where Hitler promptly killed them in the Holocaust.[3]

In 1922, after significant conflict between Jews and Arabs in Palestine, Winston Churchill set forth his government's revised positions in his white paper of June 1922. While Churchill did not explicitly oppose the goal of a Jewish state, his statement was interpreted as a setback to the Zionist movement. "Unauthorized statements have been made to the effect that the purpose in view is to create a wholly Jewish Palestine," wrote Churchill. "Phrases have been used such as that Palestine is to become 'as Jewish as England is English.' His Majesty's Government regard any such expectations as impracticable and have no such aim in view."[4] The British White Paper Policy limited Jewish immigration into Israel to escape Hitler's Holocaust in Europe. It allowed only five thousand Jewish immigrants per year to immigrate into Palestine.

Because they could not legally enter Palestine without proper documentation, and because the five thousand permits that were legally given by the British Mandate were virtually instantly gone, most Jews were considered "illegal immigrants" by the British and were rounded up in large numbers and sent back by ship to Hitler and the death camps.

It was at this time that Menachem Begin walked onto the stage of Israel's history. Begin had been the leader of a Jewish youth organization in Poland and was thrown into prison by the Russians, where he was put into solitary confinement for months.

Every day he was grilled by Soviet intelligence officers for all information concerning his activities and associations with his Zionist organization. In the fiery trials of persecution, like Joseph in Egypt, Menachem Begin's backbone became steel, and his courage became that of a young lion.

After years of incarceration, Menachem Begin was released, and he went immediately to Palestine. Upon his arrival, Begin organized the Irgun, an underground military force for the purpose of preventing the British from sending Jews without papers back to Hitler's Holocaust in Europe.

The daring exploits of the Irgun are well documented in Menachem Begin's book *The Revolt*. Begin became such a severe thorn in the side of the British that Great Britain placed a price on his head of $100,000 dead or alive.[5]

On one occasion, British officers sat in his house with his wife, Aliza, for several days waiting for "the terrorists" to come home. Begin was hiding all the time behind the fireplace in a cavity he had previously created. By removing a few bricks, he walked into the cavity, the bricks were replaced, and he stood waiting for the British intelligence officers to leave. They did...after three days and nights. Begin stood there night and day waiting for the British to leave his house while they sat on the same couch as his wife.[6]

Under the leadership of Menachem Begin, the Irgun manufactured several unique weapons in the defense of Jews being deported back to Europe. One was a delayed percussion bomb designed by the Irgun to cut trains in half at the coal car without injuring the Jews being carried back to Europe.

The bomb was placed on the railroad track. When the locomotive ran over the bomb, the explosion was delayed until the locomotive passed over the bomb; it detonated at the coal car, severing the train like a massive axe. The locomotive engine would sail down the track while the train quickly came to a halt. Menachem Begin's Irgun then leaped on the train and liberated all Jews who were being deported to Europe.[7]

The truth about the King David Hotel needs to be told. Menachem Begin is often labeled by the liberal media as "a terrorist." Nothing could be further from the truth. Menachem Begin was a freedom fighter whose targets always consisted of British military personnel or those who were armed combatants against the Jewish people.

In July of 1946, the King David Hotel was being used by the British army as a command post. British troops invaded the Jewish Agency in June 1946 and confiscated large quantities of documents. Information about Jewish Agency operations, including intelligence activities in Arab countries, was taken to the King David Hotel.

After news of a massacre of forty Jews in Poland reached him, Begin and the Irgun placed explosives from the basement through the top floors of the King David Hotel. Desiring to avoid civilian casualties, Begin placed three telephone calls, one to the hotel, another to the French Consulate, and a third to the *Palestine Post*, warning that explosives in the King David Hotel would soon be detonated.

The call into the hotel was apparently received and ignored. The commanding officer did not believe that the Irgun could have possibly placed explosives in the hotel under the noses of the British high command. The commanding officer made it very plain to Begin he had no intention of leaving the hotel, saying, "We don't take orders from the Jews." The King David Hotel was exploded, and a total of ninety-one people were killed and forty-five injured. Among the casualties were fifteen Jews.[8]

The bombing of the King David Hotel was not an act of terrorism—it was an act of combat between warring forces. Shortly thereafter,

England decided to leave Palestine, and the Jewish state was born. Mr. Begin and the Irgun laid down their arms along with the Haganah upon the rebirth of the Jewish state on May 14, 1948.

## THE JEWISH STATE IS BORN

Aware that seven Arab states under the leadership of former Nazi and British officers were about to attack them, the Jews of Palestine declared the establishment of the State of Israel on May 14, 1948, at 4:32 p.m. in a moving ceremony at the Tel Aviv Museum. The new prime minister, David Ben-Gurion, declared, "We hereby proclaim the establishment of the Jewish State in Palestine, to be called Israel."[9]

The 650,000 members of the Jewish community in Palestine were thrilled at the possibility of establishing the first Jewish state in more than eighteen hundred years. These same Jewish people anguished over the fact that seven Arab armies were preparing to attempt to slaughter them in an effort to murder the Jewish state in the birth canal.

The international community began discussing a Jewish state following the revelation of the horrors of the Holocaust in 1947. As a part of the Palestine Mandate and the British White Paper of 1922, a large section of land east of the Jordan River called *Transjordan* was offered to the Jews of the world. The Arabs so vigorously protested the land grant to the Jews that four-fifths of the property was given to the Arabs, and one-fifth was given to the Jews. It was Israel's first "land for peace" offering, and it miserably failed, as have all others that have been made or will be made to gain a momentary peace.[10]

The organizers of the ceremony for the recognition of Israel developed the plans under extremely tight secrecy, which was crucial. Israel knew that if any word about the plans leaked out, giving critical information as to when this historic occasion would occur, the Arabs would immediately either place a bomb on the site or plan an attack during the event.[11] But on May 14, the morning newspapers announced that the event would take place at 4:00 p.m. The Jewish people of Tel Aviv were so excited that they placed the blue and white flags of Israel outside their homes.

In order to preserve secrecy and safety, only a small audience was invited to the event. Foreign journalists were barred from the historic meeting.

When the National Council met at 1:00 p.m., the members still could not agree on the wording to be used in the Proclamation of Statehood. In their book *Great Moments in Jewish History*, Elinor and Robert Slater describe this meeting:

> Some demanded that it spell out the new state's frontiers. Ben-Gurion said no. Observant Jews wanted a reference to "the God of Israel." Secularists balked. Compromising, Ben-Gurion decided that the word "Rock" would appear instead of "God." What about a name for the new state? How about Judea, suggested one member? How about Zion, proposed another? Again Ben-Gurion broke the impasse: the new state would be called Israel.[12]

Just before 4:00 p.m. limousines began arriving at the Tel Aviv Museum, causing the crowd that had gathered to break into wild cheering. The last council member to enter the museum was Ben-Gurion, "all five-feet, three inches of him. His craggy face, fringed with strands of white hair, bore little expression. 'Now we are responsible for our destiny,' he thought to himself."[13]

Three hundred fifty invitees had crowded into the museum, packing the room with people. Ben-Gurion and ten other members of the cabinet were seated at a table under a portrait of Zionist pioneer Theodor Herzl. Thousands of new Israelis were listening to the ceremony via radio broadcast.

> At 4 p.m., Ben-Gurion rapped his walnut gavel three times, and the crowd sang the National Anthem "*Hatikvah*." Then Ben-Gurion declared, "I shall now read to you the Scroll of the Establishment of the state, which has passed in first reading by the National Council."
>
> Ben-Gurion raised his voice when he read: "Accordingly, we, the members of the National Council, representing the Jewish people in Palestine and the world Zionist movement, are met together in solemn assembly today, the day of termination of the British Mandate for Palestine; and by virtue of the natural and historic right of the Jewish people and the Resolution of the General Assembly of the United Nations, we hereby proclaim

the establishment of the Jewish state in Palestine, to be called *Medinat Israel* (the State of Israel)."[14]

With those words, the crowd inside the hall went wild. Some applauded, some shouted, some cried. Everyone smiled. It had taken Ben-Gurion seventeen minutes to read the 979-word document.

Ben-Gurion then announced the first decree of the new Jewish state: the British White Paper of 1939, hated by the Jews for its curbs on Jewish immigration and land sales, was made null and void. Council members then signed the Declaration of Independence.

The Palestine Philharmonic Orchestra played *"Hatikvah"* as the new Prime Minister David Ben-Gurion declared, "The State of Israel is established. The meeting is ended."[15]

This momentous occasion had been recorded by the pen of the prophet Isaiah, saying, "A nation shall be born in a day." (See Isaiah 66:8.) God did it just as He promised.

It was the greatest moment in prophetic history of the twentieth century. It was living evidence for all men to see that the God of Israel was alive and well.

## TRUMAN RECOGNIZES ISRAEL

Despite pressure from the U.S. State Department not to recognize Israel lest America offend Arab oil-producing nations, President Harry S. Truman was the first to recognize the State of Israel on May 14, 1948.

Years after the State of Israel was founded, David Ben-Gurion met with President Truman. Ben-Gurion noted:

> I told him…his courageous decision to recognize our new state so quickly and his steadfast support since then had given him an immortal place in Jewish history. As I said that, tears suddenly came to his eyes and his eyes were still wet when he bade me good-bye. Later a correspondent came up to me to ask, "Why was President Truman in tears when he left you?"[16]

History records that Harry Truman was a man of utmost integrity and highly principled. His word was his bond. He was a fierce, political competitor whose fiery rhetoric in the campaign against Dewey for the office of president of the United States in 1948 was labeled "Give 'em hell, Harry." His response was, "I don't have to give them hell; I just tell the truth and it sounds like hell."

Raised in a Bible-believing, Zionist home, Truman helped various Jewish family immigrants to come to America to escape the Holocaust. When the hour came for Jehovah God to breathe life into a Zionist state that had lain dead for nearly two thousand years, the Almighty had a man of honor and integrity in the White House courageous enough to ignore the political experts around him and to recognize the State of Israel. May God bless the soul and sacred memory of Harry S. Truman, thirty-third president of the United States of America.

## THE SIX-DAY WAR OF 1967

When the Jews of Jerusalem were forced to surrender in the early phases of the 1948 Israeli War of Independence, they relinquished perhaps their greatest treasure—the sacred wall that encircled the Temple Mount, site of the two ancient, destroyed Jewish temples. The capture of the Western Wall by Israeli soldiers almost twenty-three years later during the June 1967 Six-Day War represents one of the most significant moments in Jewish history. Elinor and Robert Slater record this event with the following words in their book *Great Moments in Jewish History*:

> On the third day of the 1967 Six-Day War, Israel launched one of its most significant and dramatic attacks, aiming to recapture the old City of Jerusalem nineteen years after it had been conquered by the Jordanians during Israel's 1948 War of Independence.
>
> At 8:30 a.m., General Mordecai "Motta" Gur, the commander of the Israeli paratroop brigade and a future chief of staff of the Israel Defense Forces, ordered his troops to storm the last remaining Jordanian high point overlooking the Holy City, the Augusta Victoria Church, which fell without a struggle. Next, the paratroopers used their tanks and infantry for a frontal assault on Lion's Gate, one of the main entry points to the Old City.[17]

Helmeted soldiers streamed into the city, some only eighteen and nineteen years old. All their lives they had dreamed that one day they would be able to touch the Western Wall. The Western Wall, part of the structure of the first and second temples, represents the Jewish people's most sacred connection to their ancient roots.

As the young soldiers broke through the gate, they crowded onto the Via Dolorosa and continued directly toward the Western Wall. "No moment of conquest during this Six-Day War was as sweet for the Israelis as this one. After a nineteen-year absence, they had regained the Jewish quarter, which had been surrendered to the Arabs in May 1948."[18]

Yitzhak Rabin remembered that day as "the peak of my life." As soldiers raced up to embrace him at the Western Wall, he spoke:

> It is with affection and pride that the whole nation salutes you today for the decisive victory you have brought us...it was not handed to us on a silver platter. The fighting was savage and hard. Many of our comrades in arms have fallen in action. Their sacrifices shall not have been in vain...the countless generations of Jews murdered, martyred and massacred for the sake of Jerusalem say to you, "Comfort ye our people: console the mothers and the fathers whose sacrifices have brought about redemption."[19]

Thousands of people who were unable to be standing at the wall that day were listening to Rabin's words over the radio. "He reminded his listeners that he had been in the city and fought for it during the War of Independence," and he described how he felt as he entered the Old City with the soldier that day with these words: "...for me perhaps the most important event that has occurred during these fifty-five hours."[20]

However, as history will reveal, "the euphoria that Israelis felt in the immediate aftermath of the Six-Day War over reuniting Jerusalem under its control and perhaps winning peace with the Arabs eventually gave way to the more civil realization that a resolution of the Israel-Arab conflict remained elusive."[21]

This day is extremely important in prophecy, for it is the day of which St. Luke spoke, saying, "And Jerusalem will be trampled by Gentiles until the times of the Gentiles are fulfilled....Then they will see the Son of Man coming in a cloud with power and great glory" (Luke 21:24, 27).

It was during the Six-Day War and the recapturing of the Western Wall that this prophetic truth became reality. In the final section of this book, we will take a prophetic look at the future of Israel—and of the world. Now that your historical foundations are established, hang on for a prophetic rocket ride.

# Section 3

# WHAT DOES THE FUTURE HOLD?

WHEN WILL THE world end? How will it end? The Scriptures are not silent about the future of our world and the events leading to the end of the age.

Jesus gave His twelve disciples the spine of prophecy in Matthew 24 as they sat on the Mount of Olives overlooking the beautiful city of Jerusalem:

> Now as He sat on the Mount of Olives, the disciples came to Him privately, saying, "Tell us...what will be the sign of Your coming, and of the end of the age?"
>
> —MATTHEW 24:3

There are ten prophetic signs in Scripture that describe the world in the last days. When these ten prophetic signs occur in one generation, that generation will see the end of the age. To begin our look at the future of Israel, I am including these ten signs at the beginning of this section. For a more detailed study of these ten signs, see my book *The Battle for Jerusalem*.[1]

## TEN PROPHETIC SIGNS OF THE END-TIME WORLD

1. The knowledge explosion—Daniel 12:4
2. Plague in the Middle East—Zechariah 14:12–15
3. The rebirth of Israel—Isaiah 66:8–10
4. The Jews will return home—Jeremiah 23:7–8
5. Jerusalem no longer under Gentile control—Luke 21:24
6. International instant communication—Revelation 11:3, 7–10
7. Days of deception—Matthew 24:4
8. Famines and pestilence—Matthew 24:7–8
9. Earthquakes—Matthew 24:7–8
10. "As in the days of Noah..."—Matthew 24:36–39

# 9 THE SECOND EXODUS BEGINS

M ORE THAN 2,600 years ago the prophet Ezekiel prophesied the resurrection of Israel from the Gentile graves in the lands to which she had been scattered, predicting the rebirth of Israel, which took place May 14, 1948. Ezekiel also prophesied about the Holy War that will take place in Israel some time after Israel's restoration to independence. In this chapter we will examine what Ezekiel said concerning Israel and what he said about the Arab coalition of nations that, under Russia's leadership, will invade Israel in the near future.

God gave Ezekiel a vision of a valley full of dry bones. I want to make it very clear that I do not believe that Ezekiel's vision has anything to do with the resurrection of the dead saints of the church. In Ezekiel 37:11, God told Ezekiel, "Son of man, these bones are the whole house of Israel." There is no doubt in the text this could only be Israel.

In a vision, God took Ezekiel to a valley full of dead bones that were very dry and scattered. This was God's physical portrayal of the nation of Israel. Israel ceased to be a nation in A.D. 70 when the Jews were scattered to the ends of the earth by the Roman army under Titus. It would be more than two thousand years before Israel became a recognized state again in May 1948—and the bones grew very dry!

God asked Ezekiel a perplexing question:

And He said to me, "Son of man, can these bones live?"
—EZEKIEL 37:3

Ezekiel responded to God by saying, "O Lord GOD, You know" (v. 3). In other words, he was saying, "I don't see how it's possible. Death has done its work. Life is gone. Lord, if these bones live, it will require the miracle-working power of Jehovah God." For nearly fifty years I have preached the gospel of Jesus Christ to audiences all over the earth.

93

I have stood in churches, cathedrals, auditoriums, football stadiums, and a preaching field in Nigeria with more than three million people attending. Yet, like Ezekiel, often as I looked over the audiences large and small, I have thought, *Can these bones live?*

In response to Ezekiel's question, God told him to do something very strange. It was the strangest message to the deadest congregation in the history of preaching! God told him to preach the Word of the Lord to the dry bones. "Again He said to me, 'Prophesy to these bones, and say to them, "O dry bones, hear the word of the LORD!"'" (v. 4).

The word *prophesy* doesn't always mean to foretell or to predict. Here it means to speak out or to preach a message to the people of God. There is supernatural power in the spoken Word of God.

Ezekiel's faith conquered the limitations of his carnal mind, and he obeyed the voice of God. It is a Bible fact: obedience brings blessing, and disobedience brings judgment. Ezekiel looked at the valley full of scattered, very dry bones, and preached this message:

> Thus says the Lord GOD to these bones: "Surely I will cause breath to enter into you, and you shall live. I will put sinews on you and bring flesh upon you, cover you with skin and put breath in you; and you shall live. Then you shall know that I am the LORD."
>
> —EZEKIEL 37:5–6

Ezekiel proclaimed that God was going to do a supernatural work that would make those dry, lifeless, scattered bones live again. It would be a reversal of death and corruption.

In perfect obedience to the word of God, Ezekiel said:

> So I prophesied as I was commanded; and as I prophesied, there was a noise, and suddenly a rattling; and the bones came together, bone to bone. Indeed, as I looked, the sinews and the flesh came upon them, and the skin covered them over; but there was no breath in them.
>
> —EZEKIEL 37:7–8

Notice that the restoration to life for the bones was a *process*. It was not an instantaneous event.

The bones were dry, scattered, and dead for a very long time. The dry bones in Ezekiel's vision represent the nation of Israel during the

*Diaspora,* beginning in A.D. 70 (Ezek. 37:11). Gradually the bones came together, and the sinews and flesh came upon them.

It was at this point of Israel's gradual restoration that people like Theodor Herzl, the Father of Zionism, began to call the Jews back to Israel. The "sinews and flesh" continued to come together as the Jews of the earth returned to *Eretz,* Israel, to drain the swamps and transform the desert into a rose. On May 14, 1948, at 4:32 p.m., the State of Israel, after two thousand years, was reborn. Ezekiel's prophetic vision was fulfilled:

> Then say to them, "Thus says the Lord GOD: 'Surely I will take the children of Israel from among the nations, wherever they have gone, and will gather them from every side and bring them into their own land.'"
>
> —EZEKIEL 37:21

God made it exceedingly clear that He would bring the Jews back to *"their own land."* He would not bring them back to the Palestinians' land—He would restore them to the Promised Land of the eternal covenant God had made with Abraham, Isaac, Jacob, and their descendants.

At the conclusion of Ezekiel 37, the nation of Israel had been physically reborn. Today they have a flag; they have a constitution; they have a prime minister and a Knesset. They have a police force, a powerful military might, and the world's best intelligence agencies. They have Jerusalem, the City of God. They have a nation. They have everything but spiritual life.

Like the dry bones of Ezekiel 37, Israel awaits the spiritual awakening of the breath of God and the coming of Messiah.

## THE PROCESS OF REGATHERING

Prophecy tells us not only what will happen in the future, but also the process by which it will happen. The prophet Jeremiah provides us with a series of word pictures illustrating the process by which God would regather Israel.

In Jeremiah 16, the prophet proclaims what has come to be known in our generation as *Exodus II.* Jeremiah declares that Exodus II will completely overshadow the original exodus of Israel from Egypt under Moses' leadership at the original Passover.

> "Therefore behold, the days are coming," declares the LORD, "that it shall no more be said, 'The LORD lives who brought up the children of Israel from the land of Egypt,' but, 'The LORD lives who brought up the children of Israel from the land of the north and from all the lands where He had driven them.' For I will bring them back into their land which I gave to their fathers."
>
> —JEREMIAH 16:14–15

This amazing prophecy came from the pen of one of Israel's acknowledged major prophets. For more than three thousand years the Jews celebrated the exodus of Moses from Egypt's bondage as the greatest event in their history. Yet Jeremiah declares there is coming a second exodus that will be so great that the first exodus will pale by comparison.

Jeremiah states that the people will come from "the land of the north," which I believe is Russia. In the Bible, all directions are given from Jerusalem. In the mind of God, Jerusalem is the center of the universe.

Jeremiah expanded his prophecy of Exodus II to include "all the lands where He had driven them." As I write this book, the chief rabbi of Israel has his representatives going to the four corners of the earth to help Jewish people return to Zion. Exodus II is far from complete, as the mighty right hand of God continues to gather "the apple of His eye" to the land given to Abraham and his seed almost six thousand years ago.

## Fishers and hunters

The Bible is a book of parables and word pictures describing principles of truth from God to man. The prophet Jeremiah puts his pen to parchment and paints a vivid picture of the human agents God intended to use to bring the Jewish people back to Israel.

> "But now I will send for many fishermen" declares the LORD, "and they will catch them. After that I will send for many hunters, and they will hunt them down on every mountain and hill and from the crevices of the rocks."
>
> —JEREMIAH 16:16, NIV

I believe this verse indicates that the positive comes before the negative. Grace and mercy come before judgment. The fishermen come before the hunters. First, God sent the fishermen to Israel. These were the Zionists, men like Theodor Herzl who called for the Jews of Europe and the world to come to Palestine to establish the Jewish state. The Jews were encouraged to escape while there was still time. The situation for Jews in Europe would only get worse, not better.

A *fisherman* is one who draws his target toward him with bait. Herzl and his fellow Zionists were God's fishermen, calling the sons and daughters of Abraham home. Herzl was deeply disappointed that the Jews of the world did not respond in greater numbers.

God then sent the hunters. The *hunter* is one who pursues his target with force and fear. No one could see the horror of the Holocaust coming, but the force and fear of Hitler's Nazis drove the Jewish people back to the only home God ever intended for the Jews to have—Israel. I stand amazed at the accuracy of God's Word and its relevance for our time. I am stricken with awe and wonder at His boundless love for Israel and the Jewish people and His divine determination that the promise He gave Abraham, Isaac, and Jacob become reality.

### "Go to the potter's house"

In Jeremiah 18, the prophet presents a second vivid picture of the process God will use to bring Israel to its divine destiny. God tells Jeremiah to go down to the potter's house, and God declares that He Himself will be the potter.

> "Arise and go down to the potter's house."... Then I went down to the potter's house, and there he was, making something at the wheel. And the vessel that he made of clay was marred in the hand of the potter; so he made it again into another vessel, as it seemed good to the potter to make. Then the word of the LORD came to me, saying: "O house of Israel, can I not do with you as this potter?" says the LORD. "Look, as the clay is in the potter's hand, so are you in My hand, O house of Israel!"
>
> —JEREMIAH 18:1–6

God makes it absolutely clear that He is the potter, and the pot in His hand is the nation of Israel. The first time the Lord set out to mold

Israel as a potter molds the clay, He envisioned that the clay pot was marred in His hand.

God did not cast the pot away. Instead, He crushed the clay on the wheel and formed it into a second pot, whereby the divine destiny of the Jewish people could be realized according to His eternal plan.

On one of my many trips to Israel, I was taken to a potter's house in Hebron. Here the potter was making pottery on a pottery wheel just as masters of his craft had done for thousands of years before. He took a lump of clay, moistened his hands, and, as he pumped the spinning wheel with his feet, he carefully began shaping the clay into the image locked in his mind.

He found lumps and imperfections in the clay and plucked them out, throwing them onto the floor. Patiently, he shaped the pot, and when it didn't come together, he smashed it and began again. The second pot came out perfectly as everyone in our group applauded.

God, the Master Potter, has shaped Israel a second time. The process continues with imperfections being plucked out and cast aside. The pot will reach perfection when Messiah comes, and the whole earth will applaud as Jerusalem becomes the "praise in the earth" (Isa. 62:7).

## BIRTH PAINS OF THE NEW AGE

Jesus presented a portrait of the end of the age and the coming of the Messiah. He presents a series of signs, including international wars, famines, and earthquakes. He makes a profound statement: "All these are the beginning of birth pains" (Matt. 24:8, NIV).

There are two facts about a woman in labor about to have a child. First, when the birth pains start, they do not stop until the child is born. Second, the birth pains become more severe and more rapid as birth approaches. The last pain is the greatest pain, and it is soon forgotten with the birth of the new child.

The world and Israel are now having contractions (wars, rumors of wars, acts of terrorism, bloodshed, and violence around the globe) that will produce a new Messianic Era. The increasing rapidity and intensifying of these birth pains can be seen on the newscasts every evening.

We are racing toward the end of the age. Messiah is coming much sooner than you think!

As Ezekiel 37 comes to a close, the prophet mentions two sticks. (See Ezekiel 37:15–28.) These two sticks represent the northern (Israel) and southern (Judah) kingdoms, which will again become one nation.

That means there are no "ten lost tribes of Israel," for God never loses anything. Ezekiel writes: "The nations also will know that I, the LORD, sanctify Israel…" (v. 28). God is performing this awesome miracle to testify to the nations of the world of His boundless love for Israel as He sanctifies that nation prior to Messiah's coming.

# 10 EZEKIEL'S WAR: THE RUSSIANS ARE COMING

IT WOULD BE sure fanaticism to suggest that the Bible mentions the word "Russia" in the text. Yet God, through Ezekiel, has made some very clear and specific revelations in the Bible concerning the rise of a great power to the north of Israel that will destroy the peace and stability of the world at the end of days.

Daniel 9:27 informs us that there will rise on the world's scene a man of supernatural power who, Daniel says, "…shall destroy many in their prosperity" (Dan. 8:25). This man will come out of the European Union and will try to resolve the Islamic/Israeli dispute now raging in Israel.

This political orator and charismatic personality will make a covenant with Israel for seven years, guaranteeing them safety and protection as a nation. In Scripture he is called the Antichrist, "the Son of Perdition," meaning Satan's chief son (2 Thess. 2:3). When the events of Ezekiel 38 open, the nation of Israel has been given a covenant by this political leader, who is the head of the European Union.

The Jewish people are confident that the European powers will protect them from any outside aggressor or invader. Israel is aware that Russia is its enemy. For years, Israel has known that Russia has been helping Iran develop nuclear weapons to be used against them. This seven-year peace accord between the head of the European Union and Israel is in the near future.

It is important for the reader to understand that Bible prophecy divides world military powers into four sectors just before the end of the age. (See Daniel 2:31–35.) The four great world military powers just before the end of the age are simply called the king of the North, the king of the South, the king of the East, and the king of the West. It is important to remember that all directions in Scripture are given based on their geographic relationship to Israel.

In this chapter, I will go into great detail to demonstrate to you that the king of the North is Russia, the king of the South represents the Arab nations, the king of the East is China, and the king of the West is Europe and America.

## THE KING OF THE NORTH: RUSSIA

Let us first consider *the king of the North* because it is a kingdom that lies north of Israel.

> And the word of the LORD came unto me, saying, Son of man, set thy face against Gog, the land of Magog, the chief prince of Meshech and Tubal, and prophesy against him.
> —EZEKIEL 38:1–2, KJV

*Gog* is a word for "ruler," which literally means "the man on top." I can't think of a better name for a dictator than Gog.

The verse tells us that Gog was "chief prince" of the land of Magog. *Chief*, which means "head," is the Hebrew word *Rosh*.[1] In his ancient Hebrew lexicon, Gesenius (1786–1842), the great Hebrew scholar, identified *Rosh* as an ancient name for Russia.[2]

In his book *The Destiny of Nations*, Dr. John Cumming said: "The King of the North I conceive to be the autocrat of Russia...that Russia occupies a place and a very momentous place, and the prophetic word has been admitted by almost all expositors."[3]

Ezekiel puts extreme emphasis on the fact that Israel's great enemy would come from the "uttermost north." It is mentioned in Ezekiel 38:6 and 15, and again in 39:2. The King James Version doesn't translate this as accurately as do the Revised Standard Version and the Amplified Bible. The Hebrew word that qualifies *north* means either "uttermost" or "extreme north." Any map will instantly verify that the extreme north from Israel is Russia.

In 1968, General Moshe Dayan said: "The next great war will not be with the Arabs, but with the Russians."[4]

Now we come to the theological phenomenon that helps us to further identify Gog and Magog with Russia.

> And say, Thus saith the Lord GOD; Behold, I am against thee, O
> Gog, the chief prince of Meshech and Tubal.
>
> —EZEKIEL 38:3, KJV

Throughout the history of Israel, God has said that He is against certain nations that oppress the Jewish people. God destroyed Egypt for their persecution of the Jews. God set His face against Babylon for their destruction of Jerusalem. Now comes a nation in the last days out of the extreme north that will attack Israel, and God says, "I am against thee." It is intriguing to note that Ezekiel is prophesying about a nation that hasn't come into existence. God says He is *against it* because that nation would be an atheistic nation. No other nation has assumed the dominant position of atheism.

All the nations prior to Russia that God opposed were polytheistic. They believed in many gods. At the beginning of time, God did not give a specific commandment against atheism. Yet His first two commandments were against polytheism. "You shall have no other gods before Me" (Exod. 20:3); and, "You shall not make for yourself a carved image—any likeness of anything that is in heaven above, or that is in the earth beneath, or that is in the water under the earth" (v. 4).

These strong commandments against many gods addressed the problem of polytheism, but not of atheism. Through the pen of King David, God covers the topic of atheism in one verse: "The fool has said in his heart, 'There is no God'" (Ps. 14:1). How utterly ridiculous atheism is!

Yet, here is a nation that will appear at the end of days, that is in the extreme north, and that will be atheistic. There is no doubt about the fact of Russia's atheistic government under Communism. Joseph Stalin said, "We have deposed the czars of the earth and we shall now dethrone the Lord of heaven."[5]

When Russia put a rocket, called the *Sputnik,* past the moon, as it neared the sun the following comment was heard on the radio in Russia: "Our rocket has bypassed the moon. It is nearing the sun. We have not discovered God. We have turned out lights in heaven that no man will be able to put on again. We are breaking the yoke of the gospel, the opiate of the masses. Let us go forth, and Christ shall be relegated to mythology."[6]

## WHO ARE MESHECH AND TUBAL?

God declares He is against Gog, the chief prince of Meshech and Tubal. Who is this chief prince? In order to identify these names, we must turn to Genesis 10 where we read about the generations of the sons of Noah: Shem, Ham, and Japheth (Gen. 10:1).

In verse 2, the sons of Japheth are given as: "Gomer, Magog, Madai, Javan, Tubal, Meshech, and Tiras." All of the names referred to in Ezekiel 38 are the sons of Japheth.

Ethnologists—historians who track the migrations of people—tell us that after Noah's flood, the Japhethites migrated from Asia Minor to the north, beyond the Caspian and Black Seas. They settled in the area of Rosh that we know today as *Russia*. Wilhelm Gesenius, a world-class Hebrew scholar of the early nineteenth century, discusses the word *Meshech* in his Hebrew lexicon. Gesenius states that the Greek name *Moschi*, derived from the Hebrew name *Meschech*, is the source of the city of Moscow.[7]

## RUSSIA'S INVASION OF ISRAEL

I will turn you around, put hooks into your jaws, and lead you out, with all your army, horses, and horsemen, all splendidly clothed, a great company with bucklers and shields, all of them handling swords.

—EZEKIEL 38:4

Why will Russia come to Israel? Let's take a look at some of the reasons for Russia's interest in dominating Israel.

1. Russia will come to Israel because they need a warm-water entrance into the oceans of the world. The Middle East offers that. Russia, under Putin's leadership, made a $50 billion oil contract with Saddam Hussein and has allowed Russian scientists to direct Iran's nuclear weapons programs to destroy Israel. Putin is the former director of the KGB who has removed the democratic process from Russia and, at the same time, charmed the West into neutrality.

2. Russia needs oil to regain its military superpower status.

> Russia hungers for Arabian oil. They must have it to regain their global status, which they lost in the crash of the former Soviet Union.
>
> 3. The mineral deposits in the Dead Sea are so great they can't be properly appraised on today's market. It is estimated that the Dead Sea contains two billion tons of potassium chloride, which is potash needed to enrich the soil that is rapidly being depleted around the world. The Dead Sea also contains twenty-two billion tons of magnesium chloride and twelve billion tons of sodium chloride. The wealth of the Dead Sea has the Russian bear salivating at the mouth.

Through Ezekiel, God said to Russia: "I will put hooks in your jaws." God is going to drag Russia into Israel. Why? Throughout its history, Russia has been anti-Semitic and, in its final form, will be led by a dictator who will lead an Arab coalition of nations to crush Israel. God makes it clear that He will judge Russia in the land of Israel, and Russia will not come out alive.

## THE ALLIES OF RUSSIA

Who are the allies of Russia who will join them in this unholy war to destroy the nation of Israel and exterminate the Jews? God gives their names and addresses through the prophet Ezekiel.

> Persia, Ethiopia, and Libya are with them, all of them with shield and helmet; Gomer and all its troops; the house of Togarmah from the far north and all its troops—many people are with you.
> —EZEKIEL 38:5–6

### Persia

Persia is modern-day Iran. As this book is being written, Russia and Iran have joined forces to create long-range nuclear missiles that can hit London, Jerusalem, and New York. During the administration of former Prime Minister Benjamin Netanyahu, Israeli intelligence gave photographic proof that Russian scientists were directing and supervising Iran's nuclear weapons programs.

There is no doubt a nuclear collision is coming in the near future in the Middle East. If Israel bombs Iran's eight nuclear sites with laser-guided, bunker-buster bombs, it could easily launch Ezekiel's war, described in Ezekiel 38–39.

### Ethiopia and Libya

Ethiopia and Libya are used in two distinctly different senses in the Old Testament. There were nations in Africa known as Ethiopia and Libya, and their names continue until today. There were also states adjacent to Persia that were known as Ethiopia and Libya. When Moses fled from Egypt because he had killed the Egyptian, he went into the wilderness, and there he married an Ethiopian. He did not go south into African Ethiopia, but went into the Ethiopia of the Arabian Peninsula where he married an Ethiopian who was a Shemite. Therefore, when Ezekiel speaks of Persia, Ethiopia, and Libya, he is speaking of the Arab states.

When Ezekiel writes concerning Russia in chapter 38, verse 6, he says that "many people are with you." He repeats that concept in verse 9: "You [Russia] will ascend, coming like a storm, covering the land like a cloud, you and all your troops and many peoples with you." I believe this is a clear suggestion that America's influence with Arab nations will become virtually nonexistent. However, Russia's influence will dramatically increase as they join forces against Israel at the end of this age.

We are watching this courtship between Russia and Iran in daily media reports right now. In an article dated June 4, 2005, for *Asia Times Online*, journalist Jephraim P. Gundzik said this:

> In the past several years a number of . . . Russian companies have faced US sanctions for selling missiles and missile technology to Iran. Rather than slowing or stopping such sales, the pace of missile acquisition and development in Iran has accelerated. . . . Russia's relations with Iran have also advanced considerably in the past 18 months. In addition to increased investment in Iran by Russia and burgeoning arms trade between the two countries,

Russia has been heavily involved in Iran's nascent nuclear energy industry. After much wrangling and repeated US intervention, Russia and Iran finally signed, in February, a deal clearing the way for the shipment of Russian nuclear fuel to Iran's nuclear power plant at Bushehr.[8]

On August 10, 2005, *BBC News*, UK edition, called Russia "Iran's main partner in its effort to develop nuclear power."[9]

What's the payoff for the Arabs? They believe the Islamic fanatical vision of exterminating the Jews can be realized with Russia's help. Absolute control of Jerusalem as the capital for the new Palestinian state will be within their grasp.

However, there is one problem looming on the horizon: God Almighty, whom the Russians defy and Islamics denounce, has brought this evil axis of power into Israel to bury it before the eyes of the world. The destruction of Russia and its Islamic allies is going to be the most powerful object lesson the world has seen since Pharaoh and his army were drowned in the Red Sea.

Ezekiel writes to the Russian leadership of this Russian-Arab coalition of nations, saying:

> Prepare yourself and be ready, you and all your companies that are gathered about you; and be a guard for them.
> —EZEKIEL 38:7

A better translation of the phrase "be a guard for them" is this: "Be thou a commander unto them." Ezekiel leaves no doubt that Russia is leading the attack.

In verse 8, Russia makes its move into Israel. "After many days you will be visited. In the latter years [at the end of the age] you will come into the land [Israel] of those brought back from the sword."

Verse 11 reveals the fact that Israel has made a covenant with the false messiah out of the European Union who promises peace and safety. But the Bible warns: "For when they say, 'Peace and safety!' then sudden destruction comes upon them" (1 Thess. 5:3).

In Ezekiel 38:11, Russia is addressing all its allies, suggesting they go into Israel, which is called the "land of unwalled villages." Russia says: "I will go to them that are at rest, that dwell safely." Why is Israel at rest? It is at rest because its leaders are trusting in their peace accord with the European Union to guarantee their safety from Russia and the Arab coalition of nations.

The wording of this verse is more than ironic. At this moment, Israel is building a massive concrete wall to keep its enemies out. Ezekiel 38:11 suggests that a day is coming in the future when that wall might come down because Israel is so confident in the seven-year peace accord with the European Union. Watch for this concrete wall to become a politically sensitive issue in days to come.

## WHAT IS AMERICA'S ROLE?

Where is America in this picture? In verse 12, Russia and its allies are going into Israel "to take plunder and to take booty." Russia is going to move militarily against Israel from the north to seize the great mineral wealth and natural resources that are there. They will promise the Islamic nations control of Jerusalem and the Temple Mount. What will be America's response to this brazen act of invading and raping Israel of its wealth? Ezekiel answers in verse 13.

"Sheba, Dedan, the merchants of Tarshish" [that is, the Western powers] will be upset when Russia invades Israel. These nations "and all their young lions" [England's symbol is that of a lion. America is an offspring of England; hence, the "young lions"] will not come to Israel's rescue. They will not send massive military forces to drive Russia and the Arabs out of Israel. Instead, the Western World is simply going to make a passive diplomatic response, saying:

> Have you gathered your army to take booty, to carry away silver and gold, to take away livestock and goods, to take great plunder?
> —EZEKIEL 38:13

What a ridiculous response!

It's obvious to the nations of the world what Russia and the Arabs are doing, and yet the Western world is doing absolutely nothing to stop them. Why won't America respond? Let me venture to say that after America's extended war in Iraq, the next administration will probably be Democratic and will withdraw from Iraq, vowing to stay out of the Middle East in the future.

America as a whole wants short, high-tech military campaigns with shock and awe that end in Washington DC with massive parades down Pennsylvania Avenue on national television, such as we had in Desert Storm. Long, drawn-out wars of attrition, as in Vietnam, will be part of our past—not our future. When America sees Russia and the Arabs going into Israel, it will be simply a war above and beyond its national will to respond. Russia and the Arab nations will form one of the most impressive military forces ever put together. As Ezekiel says, "It will cover the land."

Ezekiel makes it clear that America's and Europe's diplomatic inquiry means absolutely nothing to Russia and the Arabs. The invasion is on! This invasion is described as follows:

> You will come up against My people Israel like a cloud, to cover the land. It will be in the latter days that *I will bring you against My land*, so that the nations may know Me, when I am hallowed in you, O Gog, before their eyes.
> —EZEKIEL 38:16, EMPHASIS ADDED

God makes it clear that He is dragging Russia and its allies into Israel: "I will bring you against My land." When Russia leads its Arab allies into Israel, the Western superpowers simply watch.

I believe that after years of repeated acts of violent terrorism by Islamic fanatics such as Madrid, Spain; September 11, 2001, in New York City; and the brutal attack in the London subways of July 7, 2005, killing about fifty people and wounding hundreds, the Western nations have become gun-shy about attacking a Russian-Arab military force.

Whatever the reason, Ezekiel portrays Russia as being in complete command. Why? Because the defender of Israel, the God of Abraham, Isaac, and Jacob, has a hook in Russia's jaw, dragging them into Israel for the greatest object lesson the world has ever seen.

There is comfort and consolation in Ezekiel's prophetic portrait of the world tomorrow. The message is that God is in total control of what appears to be a hopeless situation for Israel. He has dragged these anti-Semitic nations to the nations of Israel to crush them so that the Jews of Israel as a whole will confess that He is the Lord. America and Europe will not save Israel—God will!

Ezekiel reveals a day coming when God's fury explodes against the nations that have tormented His chosen people for so long. Ezekiel writes God's description of His anger: "My fury will show in My face" (v. 18).

## THE WEAPONS OF WAR

God will destroy Russia and its Arab allies with three weapons of war that He has used before in Scripture. These weapons are:

1. A mighty earthquake
2. Every man's sword against his brother
3. Raining from heaven of fire and brimstone.

One day soon there will a battle scene report on the evening news via global television that will reach the nations of the world with these words:

> "In my jealousy and in the fire of My wrath I have spoken: 'Surely in that day there shall be a great earthquake in the land of Israel, so that the fish of the sea, the birds of the heavens, the beasts of the fields, all creeping things that creep on the earth, and all men who are on the face of the earth shall shake at My presence. The mountains shall be thrown down, the steep places shall fall, and every wall shall fall to the ground.' I will call for a sword against Gog [Russia] throughout all My mountains," says the Lord GOD. "Every man's sword will be against his brother. And I will bring him to judgment with pestilence and bloodshed; I will rain down on him, on his troops, and on the many peoples who are with him [Arab nations], flooding rain, great hailstones, fire, and brimstone."
>
> —EZEKIEL 38:19–22

When did God use these weapons of war before?

When Moses' leadership was being contested by Korah, Dathan, and Abiram in Numbers 16, God told Moses to get away from the tents of Korah, Dathan, and Abiram because He was about to give Israel an object lesson never to be forgotten in the history of the world.

Moses records the scene:

> "But if the LORD creates a new thing, and the earth opens its mouth and swallows them up with all that belongs to them,

and they [those who were rejecting Moses' leadership] go down alive into the pit, then you will understand that these men have rejected the LORD." Now it came to pass, as he finished speaking all these words, that the ground split apart under them, and the earth opened its mouth and swallowed them up, with their households and all the men with Korah, with all their goods.

—NUMBERS 16:30–32

The world is heading toward God's second object lesson. Ezekiel makes it clear that God will send an earthquake that will swallow up the enemies of Israel, just as an earthquake swallowed up the enemies of Moses.

God will use the sword of brother against brother as the second weapon of war. When God sent Gideon to destroy the Philistines, Gideon commanded his meager fighting force of three hundred men to sound the trumpets and to break the pitchers. The Philistines turned their swords against each other in massive confusion and slaughtered one another. (See Judges 7.)

God will bring this battle-tested tactic to wage war against Russia and its allies when they come against Israel. God will cause confusion to come among them as they turn and fight each other, slaughtering each other in history's greatest demonstration of friendly fire.

The third weapon in God's arsenal is great hailstones, fire, and brimstone. Two of the most infamous cities that ever existed in history were the cities of Sodom and Gomorrah. Why are they famous? Their fame arises from the fact that they no longer exist. These are the two cities where God poured out fire and brimstone because of their great sin and iniquity, and they were obliterated from the earth.

To this day geologists have sought to discover the location of Sodom and Gomorrah, but God so completely destroyed them they have never been found. Some speculate that they have been buried beneath the Dead Sea, which would explain the rare sulfuric odor and the taste of the water in the Dead Sea.

When Russia and its allies invade Israel, and America and Europe fail to respond, "He who sits in the heavens shall laugh" (Ps. 2:4) as He crushes the Russian-Arab tormenters of the apple of His eye. He will crush them as he crushed Pharaoh, Haman, and Hitler so that Israel and the world "shall know that I am the LORD" (Ezek. 38:23).

# 11 THE END OF THE BEGINNING

**W**HEN RUSSIA AND its allies march into Israel, they will be expecting to march out in victory. There will be no indication to them of what awaits them. They will have no awareness that they are making that march into Israel because God has put "hooks into [their] jaws," or that He is the one leading their armies, "all splendidly clothed, a great company with bucklers and shields, all of them handling swords" (Ezek. 38:4).

Yet, in Ezekiel 39, God has revealed the outcome of that confrontation with Israel, telling His prophet what he will do to Russia and its allies when they invade Israel in the near future:

> And I will turn thee back, and leave but the sixth part of thee, and will cause thee to come up from the north parts, and will bring thee upon the mountains of Israel.
> —EZEKIEL 39:2, KJV

God declares He will exterminate all but one-sixth of the Russian axis of evil that invades Israel. Five out of six warriors in that great army will be killed. That's a death rate of 82 percent within just a few hours. It's no wonder the world will be stricken with shock and awe.

God continues with His strategy of war by saying:

> Then I will knock the bow out of your left hand, and cause the arrows to fall out of your right hand. You shall fall upon the mountains of Israel, you and all your troops and the peoples who are with you; I will give you to birds of prey of every sort and to the beasts of the field to be devoured.... And I will send fire on Magog [Russia] and on those who live in security in the coastlands. Then shall they know that I am the LORD.
> —EZEKIEL 39:3–4, 6

This last verse suggests that judgment is coming not only to the invading Russian force but also on the headquarters of that power and upon all who support it or allowed this attack on Israel.

Notice the words: "I will send fire...upon those who live in security in the coastlands." The word translated *coastlands* or *isle* in the Hebrew is *'iy.* The word was used by the ancients in the sense of *continents* today. It designated the great Gentile civilizations across the seas, which were usually settled most densely along the coastland—just like America.

This fire Ezekiel sees coming to those living securely in the coastlands could be a direct judgment from God by hurricanes and tsunamis, or it could describe a nuclear war via an exchange of nuclear missiles. Could it be that America, who refuses to defend Israel from the Russian invasion, will experience nuclear warfare on our east and west coasts? That's exactly where most of us live today.

Why would God allow this? The Bible gives a clear answer: "I will bless those who bless you, and I will curse him who curses you" (Gen. 12:3).

Right now in America's major universities, professors, many whose positions are funded by Saudi Arabian oil money, blast Israel as the cancer on the soul of humanity. In his book *The Case for Israel*, Alan Dershowitz cites how pro-Israel speakers are being uninvited from America's universities, who boast of freedom of speech.[1] Anti-Semitism is alive and well in America.

Major American denominations are defunding Israel by refusing to buy the stock of any company or corporation doing business with Israel. It is self-righteous for Americans to point their fingers at the atheistic history of Russian and the Islamic fanatics—when we ourselves are not without sin toward the Jewish people and Israel.

How extensive will the judgment of God be upon the Russian-invading coalition? Ezekiel 39:9 states it will take Israel seven years to collect and burn the weapons of war brought into Israel by the invaders.

How many dead will there be? According to verses 11 and 12, the physical death is going to be so massive it will take every able-bodied man in Israel seven months to bury the dead. Those traveling in Israel from north to south have to travel "stopping their noses" because of the horrific stench from the bodies of the enemies of Israel destroyed by the mighty right hand of God.

## THE ANTICHRIST APPEARS

In Revelation 13, we have a description of the Antichrist, who will be the head of the European Union. This charismatic political wonder will do these things. His full résumé is given by the prophet Daniel in chapter 8.

This false messiah and chief son of Satan will:

1. *Have supernatural demonic power to know the unknown.* The Bible says he will have a "fierce countenance, and understanding dark sentences" (KJV), or "understands sinister schemes" (Dan. 8:23, NKJV). It will not be possible to keep anything a secret from him because of this satanic power.

2. *"Cause craft [or deceit] to prosper"* (v. 25, KJV). Hitler came to power in Germany because the economy of Germany was in chaos. He rebuilt the economy of Germany, bringing prosperity and pride to a nation that had been crushed by the Peace Treaty of Versailles in 1919. As Germany's "messiah," he became a monster, sweeping the world into the Holocaust and bringing twelve years of living hell to the earth.

   The coming Antichrist will come to power at a time of international economic crisis. He will cause craft and deceit to prosper. No man will be able to buy or sell anything without having the mark of the beast on his right hand or forehead. (See Revelation 13:17.) This Antichrist will control the world's economy with a vengeance. The economy of the world will flourish. Then, like Hitler, he will drag the world into the Battle of Armageddon, a literal bloodbath the equal of which the world has never seen.

3. *Make a seven-year peace treaty with Israel, which he will break at the end of three and a half years.* He "...by peace shall destroy many" (Dan. 8:25, KJV). He will be shot in the head and miraculously recover, emulating the death

and resurrection of Jesus Christ. At this point he will turn on the Jewish people. Daniel writes that he "shall destroy the mighty and the holy people" (v. 24, KJV).

The "holy people" are the Jews. They are the authors of the Word of God. They produced the patriarchs and the prophets. They are the source of knowledge about Jesus Christ and the twelve disciples. Without the Jewish contribution to Christianity there would be no Christianity.

When the Antichrist begins to attack the Jewish people, they will flee to Petra in Jordan where they will be supernaturally protected by God Himself from this monster.[2]

4. *Be a prideful powermonger.* This false messiah "shall exalt [magnify] himself in his heart" (Dan. 8:25). Revelation 13:5 confirms this by saying: "He was given a mouth speaking great things and blasphemies, and he was given authority to continue for forty-two months," or three and a half years. This demonic world leader will create a one-world government, a one-world currency, and a one-world religion. One need only be a casual observer of current events to see that all three of these things are coming into reality.

5. *Oppose Jesus Christ Himself.* "He shall even rise against the Prince of princes" (Dan. 8:25). At the Battle of Armageddon, this chief son of Satan, this false messiah with enormous demonic power, will oppose Jesus Christ Himself. However, he will not be successful! He will be bound and cast into the bottomless pit by the Conqueror from Calvary.

## WHEN DOES THIS HAPPEN?

In 1 Thessalonians 4:13–18, the apostle Paul describes the rapture when the church is caught up to meet the Lord in the air. Three and a half years after this takes place, the Antichrist, who will be the head of the European Union, is going to be given power "over every tribe, tongue, and nation" (Rev. 13:7).

How can this one man have such worldwide power and authority? There is only one reason. Russia, the king of the North, and the Arab states, the king of the South, have been destroyed on the hills of Israel by this time. Everyone who could contest the Antichrist's right to world authority has been removed. As head of the European Union, he represents the king of the West.

This suggests the following sequence of events in the near future.

1. Israel and/or America must confront Iran concerning its nuclear weapons program. If Israel and/or America is required to use military force to guarantee Israel's safety and do not crush all eight nuclear sites at one time, Ezekiel's war will follow shortly thereafter.

2. When Russia and its allies are destroyed on the hills of Israel by the hand of God, a power vacuum will exist. At that point, the king of the West, the head of the European Union, the Antichrist, this false messiah to Israel, will emerge center stage and form a one-world government and a one-world religion. For a brief period of time, he will be a one-world dictator.

3. That leaves the king of the East, which is China. China's economy is exploding. The sleeping giant is awake and has the most competitive capitalistic economy in the world. Several of my personal business associates, some of whom are billionaires, have candidly confided in me, saying, "The world's greatest business opportunities are in China." Last year Americans spent $162 billion more on goods from China than the Chinese spent on U.S. products.[3] Defense Secretary Donald Rumsfeld claimed recently that China's military budget is much higher than it acknowledges. Rumsfeld then mused, "Since no nation threatens China, one must wonder: Why this growing investment?"[4]

## CHINA: THE KING OF THE EAST

The Bible warns us of the coming rising importance of this king of the East. Revelation 16:12 (NAS) records:

> And the sixth angel poured out his bowl upon the great river, the Euphrates; and its water was dried up, that the way might be prepared for the kings from the east.

John the Revelator described an incredible marching army of two hundred million soldiers from the Orient, marching down the dried-up riverbed of the Euphrates toward Israel. Why would China make this move? China is also thirsty for Arab oil.

When the United States went to war with Iraq in 2003, China began to make a huge shift in its oil policies. Until then, most of China's oil had come from Iraq. But with the entry of America into the country of Iraq, China could no longer put all its "oil apples" in the one basket of Iraq's oil reserves. "Iraq changed the government's thinking," said Pan Rui, an international relations expert at Fudan University in Shanghai.[5]

As this book is being written, China brazenly tried to purchase one of America's foremost oil companies. Had they been successful, such a purchase could have been a serious blow to our national security.

The two kings that remain on the earth at this point in prophecy are the king of the West, which is being led by the Antichrist, and the king of the East, which is China. These two kings and their armies will meet to battle it out for world supremacy on a battlefield in Israel called *Armageddon*.

## THE BATTLE OF ARMAGEDDON

John the Revelator describes the mother of all wars—the final battle on earth at Armageddon.

> And I saw coming out of the mouth of the dragon [Satan] and out of the mouth of the beast [the Antichrist] and out of the mouth of the false prophet [the religious leader of the Antichrist], three unclean spirits like frogs; for they are spirits of demons, performing signs, which go out to the kings of the whole

world, to gather them together for a war of the great day of God,
the Almighty.... And they gathered them together to the place
Hebrew called Har-Magedon.
—REVELATION 16:13–14, 16, NAS

This passage says that the satanic trinity consisting of Satan, his
chief son the Antichrist, and the demonized spiritual leader called the
false prophet are calling the nations of the world to war. This call will
be to every nation not aligned with China. The call is for every nation
to send their armies to Israel to destroy China, the last great superpower on the face of the earth, the king of the East.

Doubtless America, Canada, and the countries of South America,
Australia, and Europe will be represented. These armies will gather
for the battle at Armageddon, or "Har-Magedon."

## WHERE IS ARMAGEDDON?

Many times I have stood on the very ground in Israel that will one day
soon be covered with blood drained from the veins of the armies of the
world.

As beautifully explained by our tour guide for twenty-five years,
Mischi Neubach, *Har-Magedon* means "the Mount of Megiddo." One
can stand at Megiddo and look across the Jezreel Valley as far as your
eye can see.

In 1799, Napoleon stood at Megiddo before the battle that thwarted
his attempt to conquer the East and rebuild the Roman Empire. Contemplating the enormous plain of Armageddon, the marshal declared,
"All the armies of the world could maneuver their forces on this vast
plain."[6]

In the Old Testament, this valley is called "the Valley of Jehoshaphat."
Joel says, "I will also gather all nations, and bring them down to the
Valley of Jehoshaphat" (Joel 3:2). Joel then describes the Battle of
Armageddon:

> Proclaim this among the nations:
> "Prepare for war!
> Wake up the mighty men,
> Let all the men of war draw near,

Let them come up.
Beat your plowshares into swords
And your pruning hooks into spears;
Let the weak say, 'I am strong.'"
Assemble and come, all you nations,
And gather together all around.
Cause Your mighty ones to go down there, O Lord.

Let the nations be wakened and come up to the Valley of
    Jehoshaphat;
For there I will sit to judge all the surrounding nations.
Put in the sickle, for the harvest is ripe.
Come, go down;
For the winepress is full,
The vats overflow—
For their wickedness is great.

—Joel 3:9–13

In the Book of Revelation, John the Revelator declared that blood will flow up to the bridle of a horse for a space of sixteen hundred furlongs, which is approximately two hundred miles. (See Revelation 14:20.) It will be a sea of human blood!

Look at a map of Israel. From the northern part of Israel to the southern point is about two hundred miles. The message? The battlefield will cover the nation of Israel!

It is beyond human comprehension to envision a sea of human blood drained from the veins of those who have followed Satan's plan to try to exterminate the Jewish people and prevent Jesus Christ from returning to earth. Yet, in the theater of your mind, try to imagine the armies of the world, armed to the teeth, representing hundreds of millions of men eager to slaughter each other.

As this great battle begins, the king of the East and the king of the West have gathered in Israel to fight for control of Planet Earth. Just then, the unexpected happens.

## THE WAR OF THE WORLDS

Before these great armies can prepare their weapons for assault, there is an unexpected invasion such as Planet Earth has never seen before.

120

It is not an invasion from the north, the south, the east, or the west. This invasion is from heaven itself.

John describes this great invasion with these words:

> Now I saw heaven opened, and behold, a white horse. And He who sat on him was called Faithful and True, and in righteousness He judges and makes war. His eyes were like a flame of fire, and on His head were many crowns. He had a name written that no one knew except Himself. He was clothed with a robe dipped in blood, and His name is called The Word of God. And the armies in heaven, clothed in fine linen, white and clean, followed Him on white horses. Now out of His mouth goes a sharp sword, that with it He should strike the nations. And He Himself will rule them with a rod of iron. He Himself treads the winepress of the fierceness and wrath of Almighty God. And He has on His robe and on His thigh a name written: KING OF KINGS AND LORD OF LORDS.
>
> —REVELATION 19:11–16

Instantly the Antichrist and the king of the East forget their hostilities toward each other. In verse 19, John the Revelator says that the Antichrist and his armies "gathered together to make war against Him who sat on the horse and against His army." It will be Jesus Christ of Nazareth who sits upon the white horse.

In this great battle, the King of kings and Lord of lords captures the Antichrist and the false prophet and casts them alive into the lake of fire burning with brimstone.

Read what happens next: "And the rest [hundreds of millions] were killed with the sword which proceeded from the mouth of Him who sat on the horse. And all the birds were filled with their flesh" (v. 21).

In the year 2006, we stand on the brink of the best of times and the worst of times. It is the worst because man's rebelling against God and His purpose for Israel makes it necessary for God to crush Israel's enemies.

> Behold, He who keeps Israel
> Shall neither slumber nor sleep.
>
> —PSALM 121:4

Just before us is a nuclear countdown with Iran, followed by Eze-kiel's war, and then the final battle—the Battle of Armageddon. The end of the world as we know it is rapidly approaching. Yet, through it all, God promises, "All Israel will be saved" (Rom. 11:26).

David's Son, King Jesus, will rule and reign for one thousand years in the Golden Age of Peace from Jerusalem. Rejoice and be exceed-ingly glad—the best is yet to be.

# Section 4

# WHAT IS THE CHRISTIAN PERSPECTIVE?

Tʜɪs sᴇᴄᴛɪᴏɴ ᴏғ this book gives you the glorious opportunity to read God's position paper on the Jews. We will leap across the mountain peaks of history and then plunge into God's prophetic future for Israel and the Jewish people. We are swiftly approaching the day and the hour when God will fulfill the prophecy of Zechariah 12:10, which says, "And I will pour on the house of David and on the inhabitants of Jerusalem the Spirit of grace and supplication. . . ."

The God of Abraham, Isaac, and Jacob is preparing to pour out His blessings on Israel and the Jewish people after thousands of years of suffering. They will be blessed beyond their wildest imagination.

# THE MAGNIFICENT CODICIL

**P**AUL'S LETTER TO the Christians in Rome has the literary framework of a lawyer establishing and presenting the principle pleas in his case carefully and accurately before the Judge of all judges. Paul's epistle to the Romans represents the Alps of theological thought. Romans 9–11 is the breathtaking and mind-stretching pinnacle of God's revelation to man.

Romans 9–11 has long been the acid test in Pauline exegesis. This awesome pinnacle of theological thought forces us to examine the historical advantages of Judaism, free will, and divine election, and to ask ourselves: What is God doing with Israel today, and why?

As we enter the twenty-first century, the State of Israel has now been gathered by the mighty right hand of God and flourishes as the only democratic society in the Middle East. How are we to treat the promises of God toward Israel and the Jewish people? Some evangelicals teach that God has replaced Israel. This is an anti-Semitic theology that refuses to believe God still has a place in His heart for Israel and the Jewish people. Something that has been replaced vanishes and is no longer heard of. It becomes extinct, just as Sodom and Gomorrah are eternally buried. How can something that's been replaced be functioning with such dynamic force and vitality? The nation of Israel dominates the news.

In Romans 11:5, Paul speaks of a "remnant." No one can study Paul's writings today without an awareness of the challenge to biblical interpretation that the Holocaust presents. Are the Holocaust survivors mentioned in verse 5 as the "remnant," which can be legitimately translated as "survivors"? In verse 26, Paul boldly states, "All Israel will be saved." In verses 25–26 he speaks of a "mystery," one that is never explained.

I am fully aware that very few pastors or Bible teachers preach or teach from this theological minefield. Why? Because the complexity of Romans 9–11 is difficult, and the verses pull us in directions we find uncomfortable. When we are compelled by a preponderance of truth to accept a position our denomination rejects, it's easier to *ignore* Scripture than to *interpret* Scripture. Paul's teachings in Romans 9–11 will stretch your mind—and mind stretching, like any other kind of rigorous exercise, can be painful.

Diamonds are not found in the dust; they're buried deep in the breast of the earth, and their discovery brings great reward. Paul told Timothy, "All Scripture is given by inspiration of God" (2 Tim. 3:16). No Christian is any stronger than his or her knowledge of the Word of God. Now, let's start digging for diamonds together!

Let's begin at the beginning!

Initially, let's understand this is not intended to be an exhaustive, theological treatise on these titanic chapters. Such a discourse would require several hundred pages to cover adequately.

There are ten basic thoughts I would like to plant in the fertile soil of your mind for your prayerful consideration. Before you throw this book in the fire, read the whole section, because the puzzle will come together. The ten concepts are as follows:

1. *Romans 9–11 is a magnificent theological codicil, which is a stand-alone document.* When a lawyer makes a will, then remembers there is something he wishes to add into the will after it has been written, the portion added is called a *codicil*. The codicil modifies the original document and becomes part of the whole. Romans 9–11 is a divine codicil by Saint Paul concerning God's post-Calvary position on the Jewish people.

2. *There are eight biblical evidences that this stand-alone document, this codicil, could not refer to anyone but the Jewish people.*

3. *Who is a Jew?* This is a very controversial matter to this very day in Israel and around the world.

4. *There is the enormously controversial doctrine of election; that God chooses to save some and allow others to be lost.* I will present why I believe this doctrine applies exclusively to the Jewish people and does not apply to Gentile believers. I repeat: Do not throw the book in the fire just yet.

5. *Has God rejected Israel?* We will explore this concept.

6. *Are all Jews eternally lost?* Not one Christian in ten thousand can correctly answer this question.

7. *Why did God judicially blind the Jewish people to the identity of Messiah?* This concept is totally foreign to evangelicals.

8. *As we examine the historical roots of Christianity,* we will discover that they are Jewish!

9. *A glimpse at Israel's future* reveals the "mystery" Paul refused to resolve in Romans chapter 11.

10. Saint Paul boldly declares: *"All Israel will be saved."* This is the final concept we will explore.

Let's return to the first concept, that Romans 9–11 is a theological codicil, which makes it a stand-alone document. A casual reading of Romans reveals the obvious fact that Romans chapters 1 through 8 represent one common theme—justification and sanctification. Every chapter is connected and flows with this specific theme.

As you continue reading, it is instantly obvious that chapters 9, 10, and 11 have nothing to do whatsoever with chapters 1 through 8 or 12 through 16.

Chapters 9 through 11 are completely unique in their theme, which is the Jewish people. These chapters are a legal insert separating chapters 1 through 8 from chapters 12 through 16. The fact is that Romans 9–11 is a stand-alone document and represents God's post-Calvary position paper on the Jewish people. Proving this point even further is the fact that Romans 12–16 could easily follow Romans 1–8 in thought and structure without breaking the flow of Paul's thesis.

After accepting Romans 9–11 as a stand-alone document, I, therefore, choose to interpret this theological document respecting the primary principles of *hermeneutics*, which is the science of interpreting Scripture. To do so we must address these things:

1. Who wrote this document?

2. To whom was it written?

3. For what purpose was the document written?

4. All scripture is to be interpreted by other scripture to avoid human error or personal bias.

We are getting ready to take a swim in an extremely swift theological stream. What is presented here cannot be my opinion—it must be the *yea* and *amen* of the sacred Word of God.

The answers to 1, 2, and 3 are as follows: The Book of Romans was written by Saint Paul to the Christians in Rome to explain God's position on the Jewish people (Rom. 11:1, 11) and God's plan of salvation for Israel (v. 26).

## GREAT SORROW FOR A GREAT PEOPLE: ROMANS 9:1–4

I tell the truth in Christ, I am not lying, my conscience also bearing me witness in the Holy Spirit, that I have great sorrow and continual grief in my heart. For I could wish that I myself were accursed from Christ for my brethren, my countrymen according to the flesh, who are Israelites, to whom pertain the adoption, the glory, the covenants, the giving of the law, the service of God, and the promises; of whom are the fathers and from whom, according to the flesh, Christ came, who is over all, the eternally blessed God. Amen.

—ROMANS 9:1–4

In chapter 8, Paul carries us to the stars with his emotional oration that nothing can separate a believer from the love of God. Then, as quickly as lightning flashes from east to west, his mood radically changes as he opens chapter 9, saying, "I have great sorrow and unceasing anguish in my heart for the Jewish people."

Remember that the Jews hated Paul. They considered him a traitor to Judaism. Paul tells us, "From the Jews five times I received forty stripes minus one," adding that he was in constant "perils of my own countrymen" (2 Cor. 11:24, 26).

Just as Jesus wept over Jerusalem concerning the coming Roman invasion that would destroy the temple, demolish Jerusalem, and turn the streets red with Jewish blood (Luke 19:41–44), just so Saint Paul felt great sorrow for the Jewish people, to the point of being willing to be placed under God's curse, if it would help his brothers, his own people, his own flesh and blood—the people of Israel.

Paul responded as Moses did when Israel built the golden calf while God was giving him the Ten Commandments on top of Mount Sinai. Moses prayed, "These people have committed a great sin, and have made for themselves a god of gold! Yet now, if You will forgive their sin—but if not, I pray, blot me out of Your book which You have written" (Exod. 32:31–32). The "book" Moses spoke about is none other than the Book of Life of Revelation 20:12.

Most Christians do not know that all Torah Jews on High Holy days (Rosh Hashanah and Yom Kippur) attend the synagogue where the liturgy calls for Jews to pray that their sins would be forgiven and their names written in the Book of Life.

## PAUL'S EIGHT BIBLICAL EVIDENCES CONCERNING THE JEWISH PEOPLE

There are eight scriptural evidences that indicate that Romans 9–11 refer exclusively to the Jewish people. Let's consider each one briefly:

### 1. Adoption as sons

The nation of Israel was made God's children, which is clearly confirmed in Exodus 4:22: "Thus says the LORD: 'Israel is My son, My firstborn'" (emphasis added). The Greek word used in Romans 9:4 for *children* is the same as the one used in Romans 8:16: "The Spirit Himself bears witness with our spirit that we are children of God."

Israel alone received the glory, the covenants, the Law, the directions for tabernacle worship, and the promises. Theirs are the patriarchs, the prophets, and, ultimately, they are the human source of Jesus Christ. Israel alone is referred to by God as "My son."

## 2. The divine glory

Only the Jewish people experienced the *Shekinah glory,* which means "the glorious presence of God." This was visible in the pillar of fire that led Israel from Egypt to the Promised Land. (See Exodus 13:21; 33:9; Numbers 12:5; 14:14.)

This visible presence of God was present in the tabernacle in the wilderness (Exod. 40:36–38) and in the temple when it was built in Jerusalem (Ezek. 1:28; 3:23; 9:3). The visible presence of God will return to Jerusalem when Messiah rules the earth from the Temple Mount, ushering in the Golden Age of Peace. There shall be no need of moon or stars by night or of sun to shine by day. The manifest presence of God from the presence of Messiah will cause the city of Jerusalem to glow perpetually with Shekinah glory.

## 3. The covenants are theirs.

The God of the Bible is a covenant God, and He never breaks covenant. Moses tells us:

> Therefore know that the LORD your God, He is God, the faithful God who keeps covenant…for a thousand generations.
> —DEUTERONOMY 7:9

The covenants God makes with His people are everlasting, without end, and actually translated "longer than forever." These covenants are not based on man's faithfulness to God; they're based on God's faithfulness to man. Those who teach that God has broken covenant with the Jewish people teach a false doctrine based on scriptural ignorance and a narcissistic attitude.

God made a covenant with Abraham, saying:

> I will make you a great nation;
> I will bless you
> And make your name great;
> And you will be a blessing.
> I will bless those who bless you,
> And I will curse him who curses you;

And in you all the families of the earth shall be blessed.
—GENESIS 12:2–3

God made a blood covenant with Abraham, giving him and his descendants the land of Israel (Gen. 15:9–21). That covenant was renewed in Genesis 17:7–14 and again in Genesis 22. The covenant was extended to Isaac and to Jacob at Bethel. (See Genesis 28; Exodus 2:24; 6:3–5.)

God gave a covenant to King David in Psalm 105:8–11 concerning the Jewish right to own and possess the land of Israel forever. Then God gave David a covenant that his "throne would be established forever" (2 Sam. 7:12–13, 16). This was a reference to Jesus Christ, who was introduced in His ministry as "the Son of David." In the future, He shall rule the earth forever from the city of Jerusalem, and "every knee should bow…and that every tongue should confess that Jesus Christ is Lord, to the glory of God the Father" (Phil. 2:10–11).

The concept of covenant is so important in the plan of God for man that it is mentioned 256 times in the Old Testament. Covenant is the soil in which every flower grows in Scripture. God does nothing, not ever, of importance without covenant. Evangelicals who teach that God broke covenant with the Jewish people can have absolutely no confidence that God will not break covenant with the Gentiles.

## 4. The receiving of the Law

The Law is actually the Torah…the written Word of God. It is a misunderstanding for Christians to call it "the Law of Moses." It is not the Law of Moses; it is the Law of God as given to Moses on Mt. Sinai for all humanity to read, honor, and obey.

When Paul wrote his letter to the Romans, the Torah had been in existence for more than 1,300 years. Think about that! America has only existed 229 years as of this date.

The giving of the Torah from God to Moses on top of Mount Sinai was where the divine and eternal met the human and temporal. It is important for Christians to remember that Jesus was a rabbi who introduced Himself as the living Torah, "Word of God."

In the beginning [Genesis 1:1] was the Word [Torah], and the Word was with God, and the Word was God.… And the Word became flesh [Jesus Christ of Nazareth] and dwelt among us, and we beheld His glory, the glory as of the only begotten of the Father, full of grace and truth.

—JOHN 1:1, 14

The Torah was given to the Jewish people thousands of years before the Gentiles knew it existed (Rom. 3:1–2).

## 5. The temple worship

*Temple worship* refers to the elaborate set of regulations for construction of the temple as well as the exact sacrificial system that would cleanse Israel from sin.

The symbolism of the temple was a physical portrait of God's plan for man. The temple was surrounded by a fence of white fabric, symbolizing holiness and separation from the world.

The entrance to the temple complex had only one door, as Jesus Christ said of Himself: "I am the door. If anyone enters by Me, he will be saved" (John 10:9). The doors to the temple were very wide, fulfilling the words of Jesus, "Whosoever will come..." (Mark 8:34, KJV).

The first item found inside was the laver for the washing of the hands. It was necessary that a person be purified before that person approached the altar for the forgiveness of sins. The laver was lined with mirrors so you could see yourself as you washed your hands. "Examine yourselves as to whether you are in the faith" (2 Cor. 13:5).

Next was the altar where the sacrifice was presented to God by the priest. It was a daily reminder to all Israel that "without the shedding of blood there is no forgiveness" (Heb. 9:22, NIV).

Then came the temple itself, whose symbolism and process of atonement are worthy of a book all by themselves. If you do not understand God's message to mankind through the symbolism of the tabernacle, you do not understand the Word of God. I have a six-hour teaching on the tabernacle that will give you a glimpse of the glory and boundless majesty of the God of Abraham, Isaac, and Jacob.

It was only to the Jewish people that God gave the temple and its fathomless revelations concerning God's plan for man.

## 6. The promises

The Old Testament is filled with promises of many kinds, but "the promises" in Romans 9:4 refer to the promises of redemption to be fulfilled by Messiah, who is Jesus Christ. Saint Paul makes this very clear in Galatians 3.

It was Moses who gave us the first extensive prophetic portrait of the coming Messiah.

In Deuteronomy 18:18–19, Moses brings to Israel the following promise from God:

> I will raise up for them a Prophet like you from among their brethren, and will put My words in His mouth, and He shall speak to them all that I command Him. And it shall be that whoever will not hear My words, which He speaks in My name, I will require it of Him.

In Acts 3:22–26, the apostle Peter explains how this prophecy of Moses applies to Jesus Christ of Nazareth as Israel's Messiah.

> For Moses truly said to the fathers, "The Lord your God will raise up for you a Prophet like me from your brethren. Him you shall hear in all things, whatever He says to you. And it shall be that every soul who will not hear that Prophet shall be utterly destroyed from among the people." Yes, and all the prophets, from Samuel and those who follow, as many as have spoken, have also foretold these days. You are sons of the prophets, and of the covenant which God made with our fathers, saying to Abraham, "And in your seed all the families of the earth shall be blessed." To you first, God, having raised up His Servant Jesus, sent Him to bless you, in turning away every one of you from your iniquities.

Moses' words established three facts:

1. *God promised to send to Israel a particular Prophet at a later time.* The language Moses uses is singular throughout: "a Prophet"…"Him you shall hear"…"whatever He says." These words cannot describe the later prophets in Israel as a whole. They referred to one special prophet.

133

2. *This prophet would have unique authority!* If anyone in Israel refused to hearken to this prophet, God would bring judgment upon that person.

3. *This Prophet would be like Moses in ways that would distinguish Him from all other prophets.* A careful comparison of the lives of the two men reveals many distinct parallels between the lives of Moses and Jesus.

## PARALLELS BETWEEN MOSES AND JESUS

1. Both Moses and Jesus were born in a period when Israel was under foreign rule.

   Now there arose a new king over Egypt, who did not know Joseph….Therefore, they set taskmasters over them to afflict them with their burdens. And they built for Pharaoh supply cities, Pithom and Raamses.

   —EXODUS 1:8, 11

   And it came to pass in those days that a decree went out from Caesar Augustus that all the world should be registered. This census first took place while Quirinius was governing Syria. So all went to be registered, everyone to his own city. Joseph also went up from Galilee, out of the city of Nazareth, into Judea, to the city of David, which is called Bethlehem, because he was of the house and lineage of David, to be registered with Mary, his betrothed wife, who was with child.

   —LUKE 2:1–5

2. Cruel kings decided that both Moses and Jesus should be killed as infants.

   Then the king of Egypt spoke to the Hebrew midwives, of whom the name of one was Shiphrah, and the name of the other Puah; and he said, "When you do the duties of a midwife for the Hebrew women, and see them on the birthstools, if it is a son, then you shall kill him; but if it is a daughter, then she shall live." But the midwives feared God and did not do as the king of Egypt commanded them, but saved the male children alive.

   —EXODUS 1:15–17

   Then Herod…was exceedingly angry; and he sent forth and put to death all the male children who were in Bethlehem and in all its districts, from two years old and under, according to the time which he had determined from the wise men.

—MATTHEW 2:16

3. The faith of both Moses' and Jesus' parents saved their lives.

So the woman [the mother of Moses] conceived and bore a son. And when she saw that he was a beautiful child, she hid him three months. But when she could no longer hide him, she took an ark of bulrushes for him, daubed it with asphalt and pitch, put the child in it, and laid it in the reeds by the river's bank. And his sister stood afar off, to know what would be done to him.

—EXODUS 2:2–4

Now when they had departed, behold, an angel of the Lord appeared to Joseph in a dream, saying, "Arise, take the young Child [Jesus] and His mother, flee to Egypt, and stay there until I bring you word; for Herod will seek the young Child to destroy Him." When he arose, he took the young Child and His mother by night and departed for Egypt.

—MATTHEW 2:13–14

4. Both Moses and Jesus found protection for a time with the people of Egypt.

And the child grew, and she brought him to Pharaoh's daughter, and he became her son. So she called his name Moses, saying, "Because I drew him out of the water."

—EXODUS 2:10

When he arose, he took the young Child [Jesus] and His mother by night and departed for Egypt, and was there until the death of Herod, that it might be fulfilled which was spoken by the Lord through the prophet, saying, "Out of Egypt I called My Son."

—MATTHEW 2:14–15

5. Both Moses and Jesus displayed unusual wisdom and understanding.

And Moses was learned in all the wisdom of the Egyptians, and was mighty in words and deeds.

—ACTS 7:22

Now so it was that after three days they found Him [Jesus] in the temple, sitting in the midst of the teachers, both listening to them and asking them questions. And all who heard Him were astounded at His understanding and answers.

—LUKE 2:46–47

6. Both Moses' and Jesus' characters were marked by meekness and humility.

Now the man Moses was very humble, more than all men who were on the face of the earth.

—NUMBERS 12:3

[Jesus said] Come to Me, all you who labor and are heavy laden, and I will give you rest. Take My yoke upon you and learn from Me, for I am gentle and lowly in heart, and you will find rest for your souls. For My yoke is easy and My burden is light.

—MATTHEW 11:28–30

7. Both Moses and Jesus were completely faithful to God.

My servant Moses…is faithful in all My house.

—NUMBERS 12:7

Therefore, holy brethren, partakers of the heavenly calling, consider the Apostle and High Priest of our confession, Christ Jesus, who was faithful to Him who appointed Him, as Moses also was faithful in all His house. For this One has been counted worthy of more glory than Moses, inasmuch as He who built the house has more honor than the house. For every house is built by someone, but He who built all things is God. And Moses indeed was faithful in all His house as a servant, for a testimony of those things which would be spoken afterward, but Christ as a Son over His own house, whose house we are if we hold fast the confidence and the rejoicing of the hope firm to the end.

—HEBREWS 3:1–6

8. Both Moses and Jesus were rejected by Israel for a time.

Now when the people saw that Moses delayed coming down from the mountain, the people gathered together to Aaron, and said to him, "Come, make us gods that shall go before us; for as for this Moses, the man who brought us up out of the land of Egypt, we do not know what has become of him."

—EXODUS 32:1

The governor answered and said to them, "Which of the two do you want me to release to you?" They said, "Barabbas!" Pilate said to them, "What then shall I do with Jesus who is called Christ?" They all said to him, "Let Him be crucified!"

—MATTHEW 27:21–22

9. Both Moses and Jesus were criticized by their brothers and sisters.

Then Miriam and Aaron spoke against Moses because of the Ethiopian woman whom he had married; for he had married an Ethiopian woman.

—NUMBERS 12:1

For even His [Jesus] brothers did not believe in Him.

—JOHN 7:5

10. Both Moses and Jesus were received by Gentiles after being rejected by Israel.

Moses fled from the face of Pharaoh [Egypt] and dwelt in the land of Midian.... Then Moses was content to live with the man [Reuel], and he [Reuel] gave Zipporah his daughter to Moses.

—EXODUS 2:15, 21

On the next Sabbath almost the whole city [Jerusalem] came together to hear the word of God. But when the Jews saw the multitudes, they were filled with envy; and contradicting and blaspheming, they opposed the things spoken by Paul. Then Paul and Barnabas grew bold and said, "It was necessary that the word of God should be spoken to you first; but since you reject it, and judge yourselves unworthy of everlasting life, behold, we turn to the Gentiles. For so the Lord has commanded us: 'I have set you as a light to the Gentiles, that you should be for salvation to the ends of the earth.' Now when the Gentiles heard this, they were glad and glorified the word of the Lord [Jesus]. And as many as had been appointed to eternal life believed.

—ACTS 13:44–48

11. Both Moses and Jesus prayed asking forgiveness for God's people.

Then Moses returned to the LORD and said, "Oh, these people have committed a great sin, and have made for themselves a god of gold! Yet now, if You will forgive their sin—but if not, I pray, blot me out of Your book which You have written."

—EXODUS 32:31–32

Then Jesus said [concerning those who were crucifying him], "Father, forgive them, for they do not know what they do."

—LUKE 23:34

12. Both Moses and Jesus were willing to bear the punishment of God's people.

Then Moses returned to the LORD and said, "Oh, these people have committed a great sin, and have made for themselves a god of gold! Yet now, if You will forgive their sin—but if not, I pray, blot me out of Your book which You have written."

—EXODUS 32:31–32

For Christ also suffered once for sins, the just for the unjust, that He might bring us to God, being put to death in the flesh but made alive by the Spirit.

—1 PETER 3:18

13. Both Moses and Jesus spoke with God face to face.

Not so with My servant Moses; he is faithful in all My house. I speak with him face to face, even plainly, and not in dark sayings; and he sees the form of the LORD.

—NUMBERS 12:7–8

No one has seen God at any time. The only begotten Son [Jesus], who is in the bosom of the Father, He has declared Him.

—JOHN 1:18

14. Both Moses and Jesus went up into a high mountain to have communion with God, taking some of their closest followers with them.

Then Moses went up [to Mount Sinai], also Aaron, Nadab, and Abihu, and seventy of the elders of Israel, and they saw the God of Israel. And there was under His feet as it were a paved work of sapphire stone, and it was like the very heavens in its clarity.

—EXODUS 24:9–10

Now after six days, Jesus took Peter, James, and John his brother, led them up on a high mountain by themselves....While he was still speaking, behold, a bright cloud overshadowed them; and suddenly a voice came out of the cloud, saying, "This is My beloved Son, in whom I am well pleased. Hear Him!"

—MATTHEW 17:1, 5

15. After their mountaintop experiences, both Moses' and Jesus' faces shone with supernatural glory.

But whenever Moses went in before the Lord to speak with Him, he would take the veil off until he came out; and he would come out and speak to the children of Israel whatever he had commanded. And whenever the children of Israel saw the face of Moses, that the skin of Moses' face shone, then Moses would put the veil on his face again, until he went in to speak with Him.

—EXODUS 34:34–35

And He [Jesus] was transfigured before them. His face shone like the sun, and His clothes became as white as the light.

—MATTHEW 17:2

16. God spoke audibly from heaven to both Moses and Jesus.

Moses spoke, and God answered him by voice. Then the Lord came down upon Mount Sinai, on the top of the mountain. And the Lord called Moses to the top of the mountain, and Moses went up.

—EXODUS 19:19–20

But Jesus answered them, saying, "The hour has come that the Son of Man should be glorified....Father, glorify Your name." Then a voice came from heaven, saying, "I have both glorified it and will glorify it again."

—JOHN 12:23, 28

17. Both Moses' and Jesus' places of burial were attended by angels.

Yet Michael the archangel, in contending with the devil, when he disputed about the body of Moses, dared not bring against him a reviling accusation, but said, "The Lord rebuke you!"

—JUDE 9

And behold, there was a great earthquake; for an angel of the Lord descended from heaven, and came and rolled back the stone from the door, and sat on it....But the angel answered and said to the woman, "Do not be afraid, for I know that you seek Jesus who was crucified. He is not here; for He has risen, as He said. Come, see the place where the Lord lay."

—MATTHEW 28:2, 5–6

18. Both Moses and Jesus appeared alive after their deaths.

And behold, Moses and Elijah appeared to them [Jesus, Peter, James, and John], talking with Him.

—MATTHEW 17:3

Then, the same day at evening, being the first day of the week, when the doors were shut where the disciples were assembled, for fear of the Jews, Jesus [after His death, burial, and resurrection] came and stood in the midst, and said to them, "Peace be with you." When He had said this, He showed them His hands and His side. Then the disciples were glad when they saw the Lord.

—JOHN 20:19–20

These are a few of the scriptural comparisons of Moses and Jesus as God's appointed vessels to the nation of Israel. It is evident that God gave promises to the children of Israel and that those promises were kept.

## 7. The patriarchs are theirs.

The patriarchs are Abraham, Isaac, and Jacob. God used them to found the nation of Israel and to birth the Jewish people, who became the apple of God's eye. (See Deuteronomy 32:10.) The Jews have blessed the nations of the world from Genesis 12 until this day, and they will continue to do so until Messiah comes.

In Romans 11:27–28, Saint Paul makes this stunning statement: "'For this is My covenant with them [the Jewish people], when I shall take away their sins.'...They [the Jewish people] are beloved for the sake of the fathers." In this verse, "the fathers" refers to the patriarchs—Abraham, Isaac, and Jacob.

Why are the Jewish people loved permanently by God? Not just because "God is love" (1 John 4:8). They are loved "for the patriarchs' sake." God made promises to Abraham, Isaac, and Jacob concerning the future of Israel and the Jewish people, and God will keep those promises. "It is impossible for God to lie" (Heb. 6:18).

There is a critical point in Scripture that cannot be missed here. In the second commandment, God takes a definite position: "...visiting the iniquity of the fathers upon the children to the third and fourth generations" (Exod. 20:5).

Then in Exodus 20:6, God takes the positive side and confirms that those who keep His commandments will have His blessing. The precedent is thus established that if disobedience brings judgment, then obedience brings divine blessing. The good deeds of the fathers add to the blessings of their children for three and four generations to come.

God has made promises to Abraham, Isaac, Jacob, and their descendants, and He must keep them to vindicate His own righteousness. Any Christian theology that teaches that God no longer loves the Jewish people or that God will no longer honor His covenant with them is false doctrine—it's simply not true, for it contradicts the teaching of the New Testament.

## 8. The Jewish people are the human source of Jesus Christ.

I have preached the gospel for forty-eight years as of the writing of this book. When I stand before a congregation other than Cornerstone Church in San Antonio and refer to Jesus Christ as a Jewish rabbi, the audience will invariably gasp as if they believe He was in fact the first president of the Southern Baptist Convention.

While living on earth, not only was He a Jew, but also He was the Jew of Jews, faithful to the Law of Moses, which, as He said, He came to fulfill, not to destroy. Without the Law of God as given through Moses, there would be no Christ, no Messiah. Jesus was circumcised. He wore the long, falling earlocks of the Hebrews, keeping His hair uncut at the corners. He would touch no flesh of the pig. He would fast on the day of repentance, would eat no leavened bread at Passover time, and would wash His hands before partaking of food while murmuring the prescribed blessing. And He would wear the ritualistic garment adorned with *tzitzit*.

Jesus was a Jew among Jews, yet the Christian gospel has so twisted truth in history that most of its readers identify Jesus with the Gentiles, whatever that may mean. However, neither Greeks nor Romans, Persians nor Syrians, expected a Messiah, and Jesus could neither speak in their alien tongues nor pray in accord with their alien paganisms.

When Jesus spoke, only Hebrews could and would listen. When He sent out His apostles, only Jews were selected. And when He gave up His soul, it was the daughters of Israel who wept for Him. He was crucified at Calvary with a sign on His head that read: "THE KING OF THE JEWS."

It was Jesus, a Jewish rabbi, who said, "Salvation is of the Jews" (John 4:22).

What does that mean?

It simply means this: When you take away the Jewish contribution to Christianity, there is no Christianity. When you take away the patriarchs, the prophets, every Word of God written by Jewish hands...when you take away Jesus, Mary, and Joseph...when you take away the twelve disciples and the apostle Paul, you have no Christianity.

Christians owe a debt of gratitude to the Jewish people that has never been repaid. It's time to confess our arrogance toward the Jewish people as anti-Semitism. Anti-Semitism is sin, and as sin, it damns the soul.

These eight evidences as recorded by Saint Paul and listed in Romans 9 verify beyond any reasonable doubt that the message of Romans chapters 9, 10, and 11 is intended exclusively for the Jewish people.

# 13 WHO IS A JEW?

T HE RAGING CONTROVERSY of "Who is a Jew?" has been a hot-button issue among the seed of Abraham for more than two thousand years. Modern Israel, with its Zionist principle of the right of return, offers to any Jewish person in the world the privilege to live in Israel and creates the heated debate, "Who is a Jew?"

> For they are not all Israel who are of Israel.
>
> —ROMANS 9:6

In the Old Testament, when ancient Israel went after other gods, every Jew in Israel was aware of the contrast made by the prophets between the nation as a whole and the remnant (Rom. 11:5). When Christ was born in Bethlehem, the nation of Israel as a whole was going about its business with little true faith. It was only a few, like Mary and Joseph, Elizabeth and Zacharias, "who looked for redemption in Jerusalem" (Luke 2:38).

When Jesus began His public ministry and saw Nathaniel for the first time, He said, "Here is a true Israelite…" (John 1:47, NIV). This is exactly the distinction Paul is making in this chapter.

Paul's prime example of a true Israelite was Abraham. Abraham was not saved by circumcision, because he was declared to be righteous before God in Genesis 15:6, which was years before his circumcision. Abraham was not saved by keeping the Law, because the Law was not given until the time of Moses, which was four hundred years after Abraham's time.

How did Abraham become a "true Israelite"? It was by faith, not works, as indicated in Genesis 15:6: "And he [Abraham] believed in the LORD [faith], and He [the Lord] counted it to him [Abraham] for righteousness."

Paul writes: "They are not all Israel who are of Israel" (Rom. 9:6).

Paul is saying there's a difference between all those who claim to be "Abraham's descendants" and those who constitute Israel as "the people of God."

Paul demonstrates, first, that Israel is a matter of election rather than birth (vv. 6–13). Not all those called "children of Abraham" (natural descendants) are actually his "seed" as demonstrated in Genesis 21:12, which states, "In Isaac your seed shall be called."

Remember that Abraham had two sons. His first son was Ishmael, born to the Egyptian maid Hagar. (See Geneses 16.) But, says Paul, Ishmael, though a physical descendant of Abraham, was not of the "seed" (Greek word *sperma*) that produced Isaac, the spiritual child.

Ishmael was reproduced when Abraham was able to have children in his own sexual strength. Isaac was born by a supernatural act of God, since both Abraham and Sarah were well past the age of childbirth.

In Romans 9:8 Paul shifts from "children of the flesh [Abraham]" to "children of God." The shift is subtle but very significant. If Abraham's spiritual *seed* comes through God's promise and power, the Jewish people are not simply *Abraham's seed*, but quite literally *God's children*.

## THE CONTROVERSY OF DIVINE ELECTION
## ROMANS 9:7–12

> …nor are they all children because they are the seed of Abraham; but, "In Isaac your seed shall be called." That is, those who are the children of the flesh, these are not the children of God; but the children of the promise are counted as the seed. For this is the word of promise: "At this time I will come and Sarah shall have a son." And not only this, but when Rebecca also had conceived by one man, even by our father Isaac (for the children not yet being born, nor having done any good or evil, that the purpose of God according to election might stand, not of works but of Him who calls), it was said to her, "The older shall serve the younger." As it is written, "Jacob I have loved, but Esau I have hated."
>
> —ROMANS 9:7–13

The doctrine of divine election is, without doubt, the most controversial concept in Scripture. It is far more complex and controversial than the prophecy matrix of Daniel through Revelation or the prophetic explanation of Ezekiel's war to be led by Russia and its Arab coalition of nations as they invade Israel in Ezekiel 38–39. That coalition will be decimated by the hand of God on the hills of Israel, killing 82 percent of Israel's enemies.

First, it is obvious that divine election is taught in Scripture. (See Romans 9:27; 11:5, 7, 28.) The question is: To whom is divine election offered? In my opinion, divine election is offered only to the nation of Israel.

Consider what divine election actually means. It means that a loving and gracious God has elected to save some and elected to allow others to be lost for eternity in the fires of hell. Now you can understand the gravity of the controversy.

How can divine election be true if God has given to all men free moral agency, which is the power to choose to accept or to reject God's offer of salvation? Free will, or free moral agency, means the ability of an individual to make his or her personal choice for or against God, and it is an indisputable fact in Scripture.

## BIBLE REASONS SUPPORTING FREE WILL

Consider the following ten Bible reasons validating the fact that God gives each individual the right to choose good or evil. Moses said to Israel, "I have set before you life and death…*choose life*" (Deut. 30:19, emphasis added).

John 3:16 is the champion verse of free will: "For God so loved the world that He gave His only begotten Son, that *whoever* believes in Him [which is an act of free will] should not perish but have everlasting life."

### TEN BIBLE REASONS SUPPORTING FREE WILL

1. Romans 2:6–16—To say that God saves some and sends the others to hell would make God a respecter of persons, which the Bible declares He is not.

2. Malachi 3:6—Adam was given a choice in the Garden of Eden. The choice was to eat or not to eat the forbidden

fruit. He chose to eat it, and angels with flaming swords drove Adam and Eve out of the garden to live under the Genesis curse.

If God left it up to Adam to choose in the beginning, then it is the same for every man today, for the Word declares, "I am the LORD, I do not change."

3. Romans 9–11—There is not one verse in the Bible, outside of Romans chapters 9 through 11, that states exclusively God's position on the Jewish people, which is that [Jewish] man is not a free moral agent all the days of his life either to serve God or Satan.

4. Joshua 24:15—There are Bible verses to prove that [Gentile] man is a free moral agent: "Choose for yourselves this day whom you will serve."

5. Psalm 119:30—"I have chosen the way of truth."

6. Isaiah 7:15—"Curds and honey He shall eat, that He may know to refuse the evil and choose the good."

7. Isaiah 66:3—"…they have chosen their own ways."

8. Matthew 16:24—"If anyone desires to come after Me, let him deny himself [free will], and take up his cross, and follow Me.."

9. 1 Corinthians 7:37—"…has power over his own will."

10. Revelation 22:17—"Whoever desires, let him take the water of life freely."

If divine election is true for Gentiles, as some major denominations teach, why go to church? Why witness? Why evangelize? If God has already determined who is going to go to heaven and who is going to go to hell, why pray? Why read the Bible?

If divine election is true, how can you say, "God is love"? How can the Holy Spirit write in John 3:16 that "God so loved the world…" if He is still going to send most of you to an everlasting hell? (See Matthew 7:13–14.)

Divine election is a fact for some of the Jewish people who are a "remnant according the election of grace" (Rom. 11:5). Divine election simply is not so for Gentiles.

## GOD BEGINS WITH ABRAHAM

Now, allow me to make the case for God's divine election of Israel exclusively. God's election concerning Israel begins with Abraham, whom God selected out of paganism (Josh. 24:2). Abraham was chosen to become the "father of all who believe." At the time of Abraham's election, he had no knowledge of God; therefore, he could not choose God.

It is clear in Scripture that God sought Abraham; Abraham did not seek God. Seeing that "the wickedness of man was great in the earth...his heart was only evil continually" (Gen. 6:5), God chose a man to be the physical and spiritual father of a people (the Jews), one who would produce the patriarchs and the prophets to write every word of the Bible, birth Jesus Christ, and bring the light of God to a world living in total darkness.

Abraham's election is easy—God had to begin somewhere. God began in Genesis 12 with the father of all who believe, saying, "I will bless those who bless you, and I will curse him who curses you; and in you all the families of the earth shall be blessed" (v. 3).

## ISAAC AND ISHMAEL

Saint Paul presents his case for election with the birth of Isaac and Ishmael. When years passed and Abraham and Sarah did not have a son, Sarah suggested to Abraham that perhaps he should have a baby with her Egyptian handmaid, Hagar. Abraham said, "That sounds like the will of God to me, sweetheart" (HAGEE REVISED VERSION).

Abraham and Hagar had Ishmael thirteen years before Isaac was born. His birth was the beginning of a family feud between Jews and Arabs that has endured until this day, dragging humanity toward a nuclear conflict in the Middle East.

Two sons...two choices!

Ishmael was Abraham's physical descendant, yet he was not chosen.

The child of promise was Isaac. He was chosen to be the patriarch of "the children of the promise" (Rom. 9:8).

There is a point to be considered in the births of Ishmael and Isaac. Ishmael was born when Abraham had the *natural ability* to produce a son. Isaac was born when both Abraham and Sarah were well past the age of producing children. Therefore, Isaac was born by the *supernatural power of God*.

This is the division between the natural children of Abraham (Arabs from Ishmael) and the "children of promise" (the Jews from Isaac).

## JACOB AND ESAU
## ROMANS 9:9–13

> For this is the word of promise: "At this time I will come and Sarah shall have a son." And not only this, but when Rebecca also had conceived by one man, even by our father Isaac (for the children not yet being born, nor having done any good or evil, that the purpose of God according to election might stand, not of works but of Him who calls), it was said to her, "The older shall serve the younger." As it is written, "Jacob I have loved, but Esau I have hated."
> —ROMANS 9:9–13

The case of Jacob and Esau is the pinnacle of divine election. Each was a pure-blooded Jew. In the case of Isaac and Ishmael, one could argue that the ancestry of Isaac was better than Ishmael's; therefore, Isaac was chosen. One could also argue that Ishmael had lived fourteen years and had the opportunity to sin, and thus was rejected by God.

Not so with Jacob and Esau. They had the same mother and father and were conceived in the same act of sexual intercourse. The Greek word *koite* confirms this.

God made His decision to choose Jacob over Esau before they were born, before they had the chance to choose between good and evil, and before they had the chance to think evil or speak evil.

God's decision contradicted the rules of Eastern society in which the younger brother serves the older. God reversed the rule—saying the older (Esau) would serve the younger (Jacob). Paul makes it very clear in Romans 9:11 that this was done "that the purpose of God *according to election* might stand" (emphasis added).

Then God makes a statement that reverberates like thunder: "Jacob I have loved, but Esau I have hated" (v. 13). What a brutal statement for a loving God to make. Why did He do it?

He did it because God knows the end from the beginning. God knew that Esau would be a wild man who would, in part, produce the Edomites, who would attack the children of Israel as they came out of Egypt bound for the Promised Land. Because the Edomites attacked the children of Israel on the way to the Promised Land, God promised to be at war with the descendants of Esau and Amalek forever, until their remembrance was stricken from under heaven. (See Exodus 17:8–16.) Esau's descendants would also produce a lineage that would attack and slaughter the Jews for centuries. Esau's descendants included Haman, whose diabolical mind conceived the "final solution" of the Old Testament—the extermination of all Jews living in Persia. It was Esau's descendants who produced the half-breed Jews of history who have persecuted and murdered the Jews beyond human comprehension.

Adolf Hitler was a distant descendant of Esau. Pulitzer prize–winning author John Toland, in his book *Adolf Hitler*, records that Hitler was part Jewish.[1] Toland traces his genealogy, which Hitler had destroyed when he came to power as the demonic leader of the Nazi barbarians.

It is no wonder God said, "Jacob I have loved, but Esau I have hated." Four thousand years after God made the statement, we have some comprehension as to why He said it. Yet the point bears repeating: it was "that the purpose of God according to election might stand" (Rom. 9:11).

## DIVINE ELECTION AND THE JEWS

Now, let's examine the reasons why I believe divine election applies exclusively to some of the Jewish people.

### A codicil intended for the Jews

I have made the case that Romans 9–11 is intended exclusively for Jewish people, as supported by the eight textual evidences in verses 4–5.

Romans was written to the believers in Rome, except for the codicil of Romans 9–11. When correctly interpreting Scripture, you must remember who wrote it, to whom it was written, and for what purpose. The doctrine of election in Romans 9–11 concerns only the Jewish people.

### An elect nation

The Bible speaks of Israel as an elect nation. Isaiah writes: "For Jacob My servant's sake, and Israel My elect, I have even called you by your name" (Isa. 45:4).

When giving His prophecy digest to His twelve disciples on the crest of the Mount of Olives, Jesus said, "And unless those days were shortened [days of the Great Tribulation], no flesh would be saved; but for *the elect's sake* [the Jewish people] those days will be shortened" (Matt. 24:22, emphasis added).

For those who believe "the elect" in this verse are Christians, please understand that during the Great Tribulation, Christians will already be in heaven at the Marriage Supper of the Lamb.

### Two nations

There is no question that when God spoke to Rebekah before the birth of Jacob and Esau He referred to nations—not individuals. Genesis 25:23 records:

> And the LORD said to her;
> "Two nations are in your womb,
> Two peoples shall be separated from your body;
> One people [Israel] shall be stronger than the other [Edomites],
> And the older [Esau] shall serve the younger [Jacob]."

Later in the Book of Genesis, a considerable amount of Scripture is written to describe the nation that Esau founded, and the remainder is about the nation of Israel.

## PHARAOH AND FREE WILL
## ROMANS 9:17–19

> For the Scripture says to the Pharaoh, "For this very purpose I
> have raised you up, that I may show My power in you, and that
> My name may be declared in all the earth." Therefore He has
> mercy on whom He wills, and whom He wills He hardens. You
> will say to me then, "Why does He still find fault? For who has
> resisted His will?"
>
> —ROMANS 9:17–19

The dramatic story of the deliverance of the Jewish people from Egypt
and the brutality of Pharaoh adorned the opening chapters of Exodus.
God heard the cries of His chosen people for a deliverer, and coming
from the burning bush with a burning message was Moses, shouting in
the court of the most powerful man on the face of the earth, Pharaoh:
"Let my people go!"

In the light of free will, consider Pharaoh's response: "Who is the
LORD, that I should obey His voice to let Israel go? I do not know the
LORD, nor will I let Israel go" (Exod. 5:2).

It is critical to the understanding of free will and election to understand that Pharaoh made a very definite choice: "I will not let Israel go!"

Those who believe in election for individuals point to the word
"hardens" (Rom. 9:18), saying God hardened Pharaoh's heart, and he
had no choice in the matter of Israel. Wrong!

God sent ten plagues to Egypt in an effort to communicate with
a Pharaoh who was spiritually hard of hearing. He refused to hear
Moses. That was a specific choice on his part.

God released the plagues in which the waters of the nation were
turned to blood. The Nile River from its source to the sea became
blood. Every bowl and dish in Egypt containing water became blood.
The pipes on Pharaoh's bath were caked with blood like blood cakes
on the walls of a slaughterhouse. You would think Pharaoh would get
the message.

Then came the frogs that covered the nation. Then gnats, followed
by flies, followed by the death of Egypt's cattle. Then came boils upon
every Egyptian, while the Jews were untouched.

151

Still, with each plague, Pharaoh said no. Hail destroyed the crops, followed by locusts and darkness that blotted out the sun for three days. Space does not permit me to exhaustibly cover the fact that the specific reason God sent these exact ten plagues was to crush the ten major gods of the Egyptians.

Pharaoh, in his arrogance, challenged God in Moses' presence by saying, "Who is the LORD, that I should obey His voice?" The God of Abraham, Isaac, and Jacob put on a power demonstration that the world has never forgotten. He systematically crushed the top ten pagan gods of Egypt so that Pharaoh had specific knowledge of the God of Israel and could make an intelligent choice based on that knowledge.

The greatest Egyptian god was Ra, the sun god. The God of Israel brought total darkness for three days, plague number nine, and still Pharaoh chose not to release Moses and the Jews from slavery in Egypt.

The point is this: with the first nine plagues, Pharaoh was given at least nine chances to repent, yet he freely chose to reject the God of Israel. Only after that did God harden Pharaoh's heart. God does not harden the heart of anyone but a confirmed rebel against His will.

> The Lord is not slack concerning His promise, as some count slackness, but is long suffering toward us, not willing that any should perish but that all should come to repentance.
>
> —2 PETER 3:9

All men will not come to repentance. Like Pharaoh, some will choose to reject the God of Abraham, Isaac, and Jacob and to follow after other gods. Call it humanism, secularism, hedonism, materialism, Romanism, Satanism, or atheism—it's all paganism, which paves the road to the gates of hell.

# 14 THE POTTER'S HOUSE

**P**AUL ADDRESSES THE word *harden* in chapter 9 of Romans.

> Therefore He has mercy on whom He wills, and whom He wills
> He hardens. You will say to me then, "Why does He still find
> fault? For who has resisted His will?" But indeed, O man, who
> are you to reply against God? Will the thing formed say to him
> who formed it, "Why have you made me like this?" Does not the
> potter have power over the clay, from the same lump to make one
> vessel for honor and another for dishonor?
>
> —ROMANS 9:18–21

Without an explanation similar to that which has just been given,
one might ask, "If God makes me hard, why does He blame me for
being hard?"

Paul offers little comfort as, in the Jewish manner, he answers this
question with a question. "Who are you, a mere human being, to talk
back to God?" (v. 20). Can a clay pot talk back to the potter whose
skillful hands shape it into its best and highest use?

There are four main passages in the Word that illustrate the relationship of the pot and the potter in the Old Testament.

> Surely you have things turned around!
> Shall the potter be esteemed as the clay;
> For shall the thing made say of him who made it,
> "He did not make me"?
> Or shall the thing formed say of him who formed it,
> "He has no understanding"?
>
> —ISAIAH 29:16

> Woe to him who strives with his Maker!
> Let the potsherd strive with the potsherds of the earth!

Shall the clay say to him who forms it, "What are you making?"

—ISAIAH 45:9

But now, O LORD,
You are our Father;
We are the clay, and You our potter;
And all we are the work of Your hand.

—ISAIAH 64:8

The best-known passage is Jeremiah 18:1–11 where God compares the pot in the hand of the potter to the nation of Israel. It reads as follows:

> The word which came to Jeremiah from the LORD, saying: "Arise and go down to the potter's house, and there I will cause you to hear My words." Then I went down to the potter's house, and there he was, making something at the wheel. And the vessel that he made of clay was marred in the hand of the potter; so he made it again into another vessel, as it seemed good to the potter to make.
> Then the word of the LORD came to me, saying: "O house of Israel, can I not do with you as this potter?" says the LORD. "Look, as the clay is in the potter's hand, so are you in My hand, O house of Israel! The instant I speak concerning a nation and concerning a kingdom, to pluck up, to pull down, and to destroy it, if that nation against whom I have spoken turns from its evil, I will relent of the disaster that I thought to bring upon it. And the instant I speak concerning a nation and concerning a kingdom, to build and to plant it, if it does evil in My sight so that it does not obey My voice, then I will relent concerning the good with which I said I would benefit it.
> "Now therefore, speak to the men of Judah and to the inhabitants of Jerusalem, saying, 'Thus says the LORD: "Behold, I am fashioning a disaster and devising a plan against you. Return now every one from his evil way, and make your ways and your doings good.""

Using these Old Testament examples of the pot and the potter, Paul makes several important points, as follows:

## LESSONS FROM THE POTTER

1. *It is unthinkable that a pot can give advice to the potter.* Hence, it is unthinkable that a human being can fault God for what He is doing in that person's life. You may not understand what God is doing, but please remember, you are the pot.

2. *God has absolute sovereignty in your life.* Sovereignty means that He can do what He wants, when He wants, if He wants, as long as He wants without explanation to you or anyone else, not ever.

3. *You are given the opportunity to turn from your evil ways (choice), but if you don't, it is just for God to destroy you.* Let me repeat two sentences from Jeremiah's illustration of the pot and the potter. "Thus says the LORD: 'Behold, I am fashioning a disaster and devising a plan against you. Return now every one from his evil way, and make your ways and your doings good.'"

If all God wanted to do was to send people to hell, He would not have taken the time and sacrifice of human life to present us with the Holy Bible, filled with messages to influence us to "turn from your evil ways."

If all God wanted to do was to send masses of humanity stumbling into the darkness of eternity, He would not ordain that preachers and evangelists proclaim His glorious gospel. A loving and gracious God has sent us a Savior in the person of His Son, Jesus Christ, calling all men to repentance. If you refuse repentance (free will), you will experience Jeremiah's warning: "I am fashioning a disaster and devising a plan against you."

If you reject repentance, look at Pharaoh's bloated corpse floating face down in the Red Sea. The world's most powerful man was reduced to fish food because he, in his free will, refused repentance to the God of Abraham, Isaac, and Jacob.

## A Remnant Shall Be Saved
## Romans 9:27–29

Isaiah also cries out concerning Israel:

"Though the number of the children of Israel be as the sand of
the sea,
The remnant will be saved.
For He will finish the work and cut it short in righteousness,
Because the Lord will make a short work upon the earth."

And as Isaiah said before:

"Unless the Lord of Sabaoth had left us a seed,
We would have become like Sodom,
And we would have been made like Gomorrah."

—Romans 9:27–29

At this point, Saint Paul quotes directly from Isaiah 10:22, which has
an interesting revelation.

Isaiah writes:

And it shall come to pass in that day
That the remnant of Israel,
And such as have escaped of the house of Jacob…
For though your people, O Israel, be as the sand of the sea,
A remnant of them will return…with righteousness.

—Isaiah 10:20, 22

Who is this remnant?

First, it's obvious that all of this remnant is Jewish. Presently in some
evangelical circles the idea is being floated that a remnant represents
the church, and therefore, all who call themselves Christians are going
to be saved. Nonsense! The idea goes something like this: "God is a
God of love, and He wouldn't send anyone to an eternal hell to burn
forever." Wrong! This is not only deception—this is a demonic lie!

The Bible says, "Broad is the way that leads to destruction, and there
are many who go in by it. Because narrow is the gate and difficult is
the way which leads to life, and there are few who find it" (Matt. 7:13–
14). This simple verse means that "many," as in the majority, will be
lost because they made the choice to refuse redemption through Jesus

Christ. There are *many* in every church in America singing "When We All Get to Heaven" who will never get there.

Back to the remnant: the "remnant" are Jews!

Let's examine the scriptural history of the word *remnant*. In the Old Testament, the word has a military meaning relating to the concept of surviving.

In Deuteronomy 3, there is a description of a battle between the Israelites, who were passing through the wilderness after leaving Mount Horeb, and the Amorites, under the command of King Og of Bashan. King Og was the only one remaining of the Rephaim, who had been defeated earlier. (See Genesis 14:5–7.) Here in Deuteronomy 3:11, we read: "Only Og king of Bashan was left of *the remnant* of the Rephaites" (Deut. 3:11, NIV, emphasis added).

In 2 Kings 19, King Hezekiah, who was besieged and mocked by Sennacherib and the vicious Assyrians, sent to Isaiah to ask him to pray for the Jewish "remnant that is left" (v. 4). Isaiah sent a letter back to Hezekiah stating that God promised a remnant would be spared from the Assyrians and would flourish for a time like a fruitful tree.

> Once more a remnant of the house of Judah
> will take root below and bear fruit above.
> For out of Jerusalem will come a remnant,
> and out of Mount Zion a band of survivors.
> —2 KINGS 19:30–31, NIV

Therefore, based on the biblical text, we have solid basis for saying that the "remnant" is a "band of survivors." What greater group of survivors exists on Planet Earth than the Jewish people? What greater *band of survivors* exists on Planet Earth today than the survivors of the Holocaust?

In 1 Kings 19, the story is told of Elijah (to whom Paul refers in Romans 11:2–5) hiding for his life from Queen Jezebel. God asks Elijah, "What are you doing here?" (1 Kings 19:13).

Elijah responded, "I have been very zealous for the LORD God of hosts; because the children of Israel have forsaken Your covenant, torn down Your altars, and killed Your prophets with the sword. I alone am left; and they seek to take my life" (v. 14).

God told Elijah to get off his pity pot and stop his "I'm the only one left" mentality, which remains a popular mantra in Christian circles today. God reminded Elijah that He had seven thousand in Israel "whose knees have not bowed to Baal, and every mouth that has not kissed him" (v. 18).

Paul states in Romans 11:5 (NIV): "So too, at the present time there is a remnant chosen by grace." We will discuss this at greater length later in this book.

The second of Paul's two Old Testament quotations is Isaiah 1:9 (NIV), which states:

> Unless the LORD Almighty
>   had left us some survivors,
> we would have become like Sodom,
>   we would have been like Gomorrah.

This quotation teaches that unless the Lord had left a remnant, the Jewish people would have been like Sodom and Gomorrah, which were entirely wiped out. According to Josephus, just fifteen years after Paul wrote these words Titus and the Roman legions would slaughter 1.1 million Jews in A.D. 70. Jerusalem would be demolished and the temple destroyed.

Sixty years after Titus, Hadrian and the Roman legions came, again with demonic hatred for the Jews, and massacred over five hundred thousand of the chosen seed.

The Jews survived the Romans, the Roman Catholic Crusades, and the unspeakable horror of the Spanish Inquisition, followed by the systematic slaughter of six million in the Holocaust. The Jewish people will survive the Islamic terrorist now attacking Israel and demanding that there be a Palestinian State with Jerusalem as its capital. Never! Ever!

God promises that by His sovereign grace a "remnant" would be saved by the grace of God, a group of survivors who have the opportunity to receive Messiah, who is a rabbi known to the world as Jesus of Nazareth.

Why do I believe that Jesus of Nazareth is the Messiah? Consider the comparisons of Moses to Jesus previously in this section, and also the following five reasons.

1. Seven hundred years before Christ was born, Isaiah predicted that He would be born of a virgin (Isa. 7:14).

2. We are told the time of His birth in Daniel 9.

3. The place of His birth is revealed in Micah 5.

4. The intimate details of His life and death are recorded in Psalm 22 and Isaiah 53.

5. The fact of His resurrection is stated in Psalm 16.

The only person in human history who connects all these dots is Rabbi Jesus Christ of Nazareth.

## CHRIST THE STUMBLING STONE
## ROMANS 9:32–33

For they stumbled at that stumbling stone. As it is written:

"Behold, I lay in Zion a stumbling stone and rock of offense,
And whoever believes on Him will not be put to shame."
—ROMANS 9:32–33

Saint Paul closes Romans 9 with two quotations from Isaiah 8:14 and 28:16. As I stated at the beginning of Section Four, the only way to accurately interpret scripture is by other scripture. Paul does that to prove to his audience that Jesus of Nazareth is a stumbling stone to the Jewish people.

He will be as a sanctuary,
But a stone of stumbling and a rock of offense
To both the houses of Israel,
As a trap and a snare to the inhabitants of Jerusalem.
—ISAIAH 8:14

Behold, I lay in Zion a stone for a foundation,
A tried stone, a precious cornerstone, a sure foundation;
Whoever believes will not act hastily.
—ISAIAH 28:16

In Isaiah 8:14, Isaiah is saying that Jehovah is a stone that causes people to stumble. In Isaiah 28:16, the prophet makes it clear that the stumbling stone is another individual whom God is going to send out of Zion. That stumbling stone was Jesus Christ, sent by Jehovah God to the world in Bethlehem's manger.

Saint Paul teaches in 1 Corinthians 1:20–25, 27–29 that the gospel of Jesus Christ was weakness to the Romans. The Romans worshiped power! Might makes right! A King dying on a cross with criminals was weakness—not power.

According to Paul, the cross was foolishness to the Greeks. The Greeks admired beauty and culture. There was nothing beautiful about a Roman crucifixion. It was an unspeakable process of torture that left a disfigured human body, a blood-soaked mass of twisted flesh.

To the Jewish people, the cross was a stumbling stone. Some of the Jews wanted a Messiah of power to crush Roman oppression. They were not looking for a rabbi teaching, "Blessed are the meek for they shall inherit the earth." You couldn't stop Rome with meekness—get a sword.

## MORE CAUSES FOR OFFENSE

The Jewish people were seeking a sign that Jesus was the Messiah. To the Jews who sought signs, the cross of Christ was a "stumbling stone" (1 Cor. 1:22–23). The signs the Jews looked for were not signs and wonders, because there were plenty of those. They were looking for signs that Jesus was the Messiah.

According to the Torah, a crucified man is "accursed of God" (Deut. 21:23, KJV). It was the way Jesus died that failed to meet the Jewish expectation for a "sign of Messiah."

The deity of Jesus Christ was and is a stumbling stone to Israel and the world. But there are other "stumbling stones."

Consider that a stone is a *lowly* thing, as illustrated by Jesus' life. He was born in a manger to a carpenter, lived in Nazareth, and socialized with the poorest of the poor. He ate with sinners. By Rome, He was considered to be an insurrectionist too dangerous to live. The Pharisees called him a drunkard, a man who socialized with sinners and performed miracles by the power of the devil. Jesus simply didn't know the right people and was considered to be an angry, radical, right-winger, driving the moneychangers out of the temple and surrounding Himself with twelve men of little distinction, one of whom tried to betray Him to the Roman government.

Isaiah stated:

> He has no form or comeliness;
> And when we see Him,
> There is no beauty that we should desire Him.
> He is despised and rejected by men,
> A Man of sorrows and acquainted with grief.
>
> —Isaiah 53:2–3

The point is this: a stone that causes someone to stumble is not one that is placed in some high position in the construction of the synagogue. The "stumbling stone" is one that's neglected, one that lies without notice in the grass on the ground where men trip over it and stumble when they come upon it suddenly.

There is an important issue concerning this stumbling stone. *It becomes the capstone.* King David points this out in Psalm 118:22, saying: "The stone the builders rejected has become the capstone" (NIV). Jesus quoted this verse from Psalm 118 when the religious leaders were looking for a way to arrest Him. Jesus said:

> Have you never read in the Scriptures:
>
> "The stone the builders rejected
>    has become the capstone;
> the Lord has done this,
>    and it is marvelous in our eyes"?
>
> —Matthew 21:42, NIV; cf. Mark 12:10–11; Luke 20:17

When Peter and John were put on trial before the Sanhedrin, following Jesus' resurrection and ascension, Peter told the religious leaders:

> Jesus Christ of Nazareth...is the stone which was rejected by you builders, which has become the chief cornerstone.
>
> —Acts 4:10–11

There is a Catholic doctrine that presents Peter as the foundation of the church. This is simply not true according to the eternal, inherent Word of God.

Jesus told Peter: "You are Peter [the Greek word here for Peter is *Petros*, which means a piece of a rock or something as small as a pebble for a boy's slingshot], and on this rock [Jesus says pointing to Himself] I will build My church, and the gates of Hades shall not prevail against it" (Matt. 16:18).

The Greek word for rock when Jesus was speaking of Himself is *petra*, which means "bedrock."

Jesus was saying to Peter, "You are a little pebble in a boy's slingshot, *Petros*, but I'm going to build My church on Myself, because I am the bedrock, the *petra*."

The idea that the Roman Catholic pope speaks as the voice of God with infallibility because he, as the pope, is an extension of Saint Peter is a terrible twisting of Scripture. Peter is a pebble; Jesus Christ is the bedrock who said, "Upon this rock I will build my church; and the gates of hell shall not prevail against it" (Matt. 16:18, KJV).

## SHALL NOT BE ASHAMED
## ROMANS 9:33

Whoever believes on Him will not be put to shame.

—ROMANS 9:33

Saint Paul closes chapter 9 by saying, "The one who puts his trust in Jesus Christ will not be humiliated or put to shame on the Day of Judgment."

Picture yourself standing before God as, from the Book of Life, every word, thought, and deed of your life is being read aloud for all humanity to hear—knowing you have rejected Christ. You are fully aware that your judgment is so horrible that you wish the mountains would fall on you to protect you from the wrath of God. On that day, without Christ, you will certainly be humiliated and ashamed.

If you are standing firmly on the solid rock, you will be without a trace of shame or humiliation. Is Christ a stumbling stone to you, or have you accepted Him as the Cornerstone, precious and elect in Zion as the foundation of your life?

The first two verses of Romans 10 are linked to the last two verses of Romans 9, and it makes the first two verses of Romans 10 so very compelling. Saint Paul opens chapter 10 with a compassionate prayer for his fellow Jews.

Remember that chapter 10, as is true also of chapters 9 and 11, concerns the Jewish people. This three-chapter document is God's position paper on His chosen people.

Paul's prayer for Israel is that "they may be saved" (Rom. 10:1). The Greek word used here is *soteria*, indicating that Paul is praying that his fellow Jews will be gathered into the people that God is now forming on the basis of faith in the Messiah. Salvation here does not mean that the Jewish people will run down and join the Christian church on the corner. They didn't do that for Martin Luther, and they won't do that in the future. Paul is praying for a spiritual awakening among the Jewish people, one that gathers them into "the elect" that God is bringing together as evidenced by Romans 11:5. I believe that God is now gathering the 144,000 Jews who will carry God's message to the nations as recorded in Revelation 7:4–8.

Paul testifies that the Jewish people have a "zeal for God" (Rom. 10:2).

Paul testified that he was so zealous for Judaism that he threw Christians into prison where some were killed (Phil. 3:6). Paul was a poster child for being zealous for his faith as a Jew.

On the road to Damascus, Paul had a divine revelation of Rabbi Jesus Christ of Nazareth, and the Bible says, "There fell from his eyes something like scales" (Acts 9:18). I'll explain the scriptural importance of this verse in our discussion of Romans 11.

# HAS GOD REJECTED ISRAEL?

THE CONCEPT OF replacement theology is popular in America's churches. *Replacement theology* means that Israel failed, and God has replaced Israel with the church. This is simply not true.

> I say then, has God cast away His people? Certainly not! For I also am an Israelite, of the seed of Abraham, of the tribe of Benjamin.
>
> —ROMANS 11:1

Twice in Romans 11 Paul says that Israel has not fallen and is still the apple of God's eye. (See Romans 11:1, 11.) In the New Testament, the word *Israel* is used seventy-seven times. Clearly, in seventy-one of those references it speaks of the nation of Israel, which is 96 percent of the time. It does not refer to the church.

Has God cast away Israel? Absolutely not! The fact is, when something is "cast away," you never hear of it again. Yet in the Book of Revelation, twelve tribes of Israel, and twelve thousand out of each of the twelve tribes, are sealed to present the gospel during the Great Tribulation (Rev. 7:4).

Let me remind you that during the Great Tribulation the Gentile church is in heaven. The 144,000 who will be sealed to present the gospel to the world will be 144,000 Jewish people who have a supernatural revelation of the identity of Jesus Christ as Messiah, similar to Saint Paul's revelation on the road to Damascus. The point here is that a nation called *Israel* is alive and well during the Tribulation. They will be part of the first matter of business when Christ returns to earth—the judgment of the nations. And the basis for this judgment is to be how the nations of the world treated the Jewish people and the nation of Israel. (See Matthew 25:31–46.)

The point is simply this: if God has cast away Israel, why do they still exist in the Book of Revelation? Why does God have a judgment of nations to judge all nations and men for the way in which they treated the Jewish people from Genesis to the Second Coming?

Two pictures of Abraham's seed that clearly reflect the difference between Israel and the church can be found in Scripture.

The first picture of Abraham's seed presents Abraham's descendants as "the sand of the sea." (See Genesis 22:17; Hebrews 11:12.) Sand is earthy. Its volume represents the multitudes of people from Abraham's seed—both Jews and Arabs.

The second picture of Abraham's seed, found in the same Scripture verses, is as "the stars of the heavens."

The stars of the heavens represent the church. The features of the stars are as follows:

1. The stars produce light, and the church is commanded to be "the light of the world."

2. The stars rule the night, just as the church is commanded to rule over powers and principalities of darkness.

3. The church rules in heavenly places, which, as reflected in Ephesians 6, is the role of the church.

4. God gave to the Jewish people a physical land whose literal boundaries are given in Genesis 15:18–21. It is a specific land with Jerusalem as its capital city forever. The church has been given a heavenly kingdom, just as Christ promised: "In My Father's house [heaven] are many mansions....I will come again and receive you to Myself; that where I am [with the Father in heaven], there you may be also" (John 14:2–3).

Israel has been given an earthly kingdom with an earthly Jerusalem now located in Israel. The church has been given the New Jerusalem located in heaven.

The only way anyone can confuse the obvious meaning of Scripture is to "spiritualize" the text with an allegorical meaning rather than a factual meaning. That's why scriptures must be interpreted by other scriptures, paying close attention to whom it is written and for what

purpose, lest it become twisted and distorted by theological demagogues, leading to confusion and deception.

The point of these pictures is this: stars are heavenly, and sand is
earthly. They are unique and very different. One never replaces the
other. The stars have their role, and the sand has its role, but they never
interact.

## A JEWISH REMNANT
## ROMANS 11:2–5

> God has not cast away His people whom He foreknew. Or do
> you not know what the Scripture says of Elijah, how he pleads
> with God against Israel, saying, "LORD, they have killed Your
> prophets and torn down Your altars, and I alone am left, and
> they seek my life"? But what does the divine response say to him?
> "I have reserved for Myself seven thousand men who have not
> bowed the knee to Baal." Even so then, at this present time there
> is a *remnant according to the election of grace.*
>                   —ROMANS 11:2–5, EMPHASIS ADDED

Paul validates that God has not cast Israel away, because Paul is Jewish, of the tribe of Benjamin, and he, at the very least, represents a
"remnant of one." Paul's logic is this: if there is just one Jew in this elect
remnant, then God has not rejected Israel.

Paul expands the picture with the story of the prophet Elijah. Elijah
challenged the priests of Baal to call fire down from heaven to consume
the sacrifice. When the priests of Baal failed, and the God of Abraham, Isaac, and Jacob consumed the sacrifice with such an all-consum-
ing fire that it devoured the sacrifice, the wood, the stones, the soil,
and the water in the trench around the sacrifice, Elijah then killed four
hundred fifty prophets of Baal, concluding the camp meeting services
at the crest of Mount Carmel.

When Queen Jezebel heard the news, she swore to kill Elijah immediately in swift retaliation. Elijah, exhausted and depressed, fled for
his life into the Sinai wilderness.

The next morning, God asked Elijah, "What are you doing here,
Elijah?"

Elijah replied, "Lord, they have killed Your prophets, and they have demolished Your altars. I am the last one left, and they want to kill me." (See 1 Kings 19.)

Listen closely to God's response to Elijah's depressed response: "I have kept for Myself seven thousand men who have not bent the knee to Baal." (See verse 18.)

Fact: Elijah, as the prophet, should have known those seven thousand faithful followers of Jehovah God. There was a far greater group in the remnant of Israel than Elijah knew or imagined when he gave his "I am the last one left standing" speech.

Saint Paul then builds on Elijah's story, writing, "Even so then, at this present time there is a remnant [of surviving Jews] according to the election of grace" (Rom. 11:5).

Notice Paul's progression of thought:

1. Romans 9:27 declares that a "remnant will be saved."

2. Romans 9:25–26 states that not *all* Jewish people would be saved, and *some* Gentiles would be.

3. Romans 11:1 validates that God has not rejected Israel.

4. In the end, "All Israel will be saved" (Rom. 11:26).

God has always preserved a surviving remnant of Jewish people, and, as per Elijah, the remnant is probably much larger than many spiritual leaders think. When we read, "All Israel will be saved," in Romans 11:26, we have progressed from a remnant of one (Saint Paul, v. 1) to a remnant of seven thousand (v. 4), to the shocking proclamation, "All Israel will be saved" (v. 26). God's Word paints the portrait that Israel's future is secure and bright.

Paul makes it crystal clear in Romans 11:6 that this divine election is by grace alone. Both Christians and Jews are guilty of trying to establish their righteousness by works. Works may reflect your love for God, but in no way do they make you righteous. The Bible says, "There is none righteous, no, not one" (Rom. 3:10).

I was raised in the home of a devout Pentecostal pastor who served in the kingdom of God for forty years with distinction and accomplishment. However, we had more rules than the IRS. Those silly, man-made, religious rules were preached under the banner of "holiness." Some of those rules were:

- Thou shall not go to movies.

- Thou shall not play cards, dominoes, or Monopoly. Why Monopoly? Because Monopoly had dice, and we were forbidden even to have "the appearance of evil."

- Thou shall not go to any dance—as a matter of fact, don't shuffle your feet while singing the hymns, or you will be accused of dancing.

- Thou shall not go to ball games. Why? Because at ball games they sell beer, and the cheerleaders have short dresses, and you might be corrupted.

- Thou shall not date anyone who is not Pentecostal.

- Thou shall not associate with the world for any reason. Forget that Jesus Christ ate with tax collectors and prostitutes—you must separate yourself from the world.

If I took the time and space to list all of those silly rules, you wouldn't believe it.

If you kept all these stupid rules in this particular brand of Pentecostalism, you were considered "holy." Forget that you might have had a tongue sharp enough to trim a hedge. Forget your loveless nature and your unforgiving spirit from which Hitler could learn. You were considered "holy" if you kept these rules. It was wrong in the Old Testament. It was wrong in Pentecostalism. It will always be wrong.

You are not made holy by keeping man-made rules to obtain righteousness with God. That is legalism—and God hates legalism with a passion. Why? Because if you could keep a set of rules and thereby become "holy," your works are the source of your salvation.

You are made righteous by the atonement of the cross. In Scripture, salvation is very simple: "Believe on the Lord Jesus Christ, and you will be saved." Forget the encyclopedia of man-made religious rules! Burn it! You are made holy by the work of the cross.

## DIVINE BLINDNESS
## ROMANS 11:7–10

What then? Israel has not obtained what it seeks; but the elect have obtained it, and *the rest were blinded.* Just as it is written:

"God has given them a spirit of stupor,
Eyes that they should not see
And ears that they should not hear,
To this very day."

And David says:

"Let their table become a snare and a trap,
A stumbling block and a recompense to them.
Let their eyes be darkened, so that they do not see,
And bow down their back always."
—ROMANS 11:7–10, EMPHASIS ADDED

Paul now covers the topic of God, by His own hand, causing divine blindness concerning the identity of Messiah to come upon the Jewish people. The fact that the Jewish people were blinded to the identity of Messiah is verified three times in Romans 11: "...the rest were blinded" (v. 7); "Let their eyes be darkened, so that they do not see" (v. 10); and "...blindness in part has happened to Israel until the fullness of the Gentiles has come in" (v. 25).

Romans 11:32 states: "For God has committed them all to disobedience." This verse means that God locked the Jewish people up in unbelief.

Paul continued writing about the blindness of the Jewish people concerning the true identity of Christ in 2 Corinthians 3:12–15:

Therefore, since we have such hope, we use great boldness of speech—unlike Moses, who put a veil over his face so that the children of Israel could not look steadily at the end of what was passing away. But their minds were blinded. For until this day the same veil remains unlifted in the reading of the Old Testament, because the veil is taken away in Christ. But even to this day, when Moses is read, a veil lies on their heart.

A critical question to ask at this point is: When did this spiritual blindness begin?

Scripture is very clear that this spiritual blindness began when Moses was leading the children of Israel out of Egypt to the Promised Land. He had been their leader for forty years, and he made this astonishing statement to the Jewish people.

> Now Moses called all Israel and said to them: "You have seen all that the LORD did before your eyes in the land of Egypt, to Pharaoh and to all his servants and to all his land—the great trials which your eyes have seen, the signs, and those great wonders. [Now listen to what Moses says next.] Yet the LORD has not given you a heart to perceive and *eyes to see* and *ears to hear* to this very day."
> —DEUTERONOMY 29:2–4, EMPHASIS ADDED

This spiritual blindness and deafness continued and is confirmed by the prophet Isaiah, who wrote:

> And He [God] said, "Go, and tell this people:
>
> 'Keep on hearing, but do not understand;
> Keep on seeing, but do not perceive.'
>
> Make the heart of this people dull,
> And their ears heavy,
> And shut their eyes;
> Lest they see with their eyes,
> And hear with their ears."
> —ISAIAH 6:9–10, EMPHASIS ADDED

Jesus of Nazareth made it clear to His twelve disciples why He taught the Jewish people in parables. Christ's answer is shocking and contains a major revelation.

> And the disciples came and said to Him, "Why do You speak to them in parables?" He [Jesus] answered and said to them, "Because it has been given to you [the disciples] to know the mysteries of the kingdom of heaven [this is revelation], but to them it has not been given.... Therefore I speak to them in parables, because seeing they do not see [because of spiritual blindness], and hearing they do not hear, nor do they understand.

And in them the prophecy of Isaiah is fulfilled."

—MATTHEW 13:10–14

Again, Saint Paul confirms that this God-given blindness to the identity of Messiah is still in place twenty years after the cross: "that blindness in part has happened to Israel until the fullness of the Gentiles has come in" (Rom. 11:25).

When will this blindness end? The blindness to the identity of Messiah as a nation will remain as long as the Gentile church is in the world. Notice both Moses and Isaiah said Jewish ears were spiritually deaf. The point is this. The Bible says, "Faith comes by hearing, and hearing by the word of God" (Rom. 10:17). If God caused the Jewish people to be deaf to hearing the gospel, what are their options?

In the story of Joseph, God has made it very clear how and when this God-given blindness will end. Remember that the Old Testament is *God's will concealed*, and the New Testament is *God's will revealed*. Let's examine the lives of Joseph and Jesus in Scripture:

## PARALLELS BETWEEN JOSEPH AND JESUS

1. The names of Joseph and Jesus come from the same Hebrew root word.

2. Joseph was the favorite son of his father. Jesus was the only begotten Son of His Father.

3. Joseph had a coat of many colors, representing royalty. Jesus had a seamless coat so valuable that Roman soldiers gambled for it at the foot of the cross, where He was hung as "King of the Jews."

4. Joseph was sent to his brothers in the field with food. Jesus was sent by His Father to Earth as the bread of life, as living water, as milk for spiritual infants and meat for men.

5. Joseph was rejected by his brothers and sold to the Midianites, who carried him to Egypt. Jesus "came unto His own and His own received him not," and was sold by Judas for thirty pieces of silver.

6. Joseph was falsely accused of rape by Potiphar's wife and sent to prison. Jesus Christ was falsely accused by the Pharisees as being demonized, a drunkard, and a heretic. For this He was executed by Rome and entered the prison of death.

7. Joseph came out of prison and instantly became prime minister of Egypt, standing at the right hand of the most powerful man on earth—Pharaoh. Jesus came out of the prison of death and instantly ascended into heaven, standing at the right hand of God the Father, the most powerful force in the universe.

8. Hunger and starvation drove Joseph's brothers into Egypt to see the brother they rejected and did not know. Joseph was dressed as an Egyptian; he spoke as an Egyptian and was married to a Gentile wife with two sons, Manasseh and Ephraim.

   Joseph's wife represents the Gentile church, and his two sons, their spiritual offspring. It is to be remembered that Manasseh and Ephraim were given a full inheritance with national Israel.

   Remember that Joseph did not reveal himself to his brothers until the Gentiles were removed from the room. This means to me that Christ will not reveal Himself to the Jewish people until after the rapture when the church has been removed from the earth.

Another mystery in the story of Joseph and his brothers is that Joseph set his brothers at the banquet table in the order of their birth. Only Joseph could know that natural order. This means to me that God is now calling the Jews of the world back to Israel so that a significant representation of each of the twelve tribes is home. God will call 144,000 Jews (12,000 out of each the twelve tribes) to carry the message of heaven to the four corners of the earth in the Tribulation Era.

Joseph's brothers came into Egypt three times seeking food before Joseph revealed himself to them as their flesh and blood. The Jewish people have now entered the Promised Land of Israel for the third time. The first time they came with Joshua, the second time with Nehemiah to rebuild the wall, and the third time they came was on May 14, 1948, when the nation of Israel was reborn in the greatest prophetic miracle of the ages.

On the third time into the land, the revelation of Joseph's real identity was made known to his brothers. Now that the Jewish people, the family of Jesus Christ, have entered Israel for the third time, His true identity will be made known in the near future.

What did Joseph's brothers do when they saw Joseph's circumcision (which Egyptians did not have) and knew beyond any shadow of doubt that Joseph was indeed flesh of their flesh and bone of their bone? They fell on each other's shoulders and wept so loudly it was heard throughout Joseph's palace. They wept without consolation.

What does the prophet Zechariah say will happen when the Jewish people in the near future recognize that Jesus is indeed their Joseph? Listen to Zechariah's description:

> And I will pour on the house of David and on the inhabitants of Jerusalem the Spirit of grace and supplication; then they will look on Me whom they pierced. Yes, they will mourn for Him as one mourns for his only son, and grieve for him as one grieves for a firstborn.
>
> —Zechariah 12:10

When will the divinely imparted spiritual blindness upon the Jewish people end concerning the identity of Jesus Christ as Messiah? This spiritual blindness will end when Christ returns to Earth and they see the scars in His hands from the Roman crucifixion.

Is this blindness given to all the Jewish people? The answer is absolutely not! That brings us to the next concept.

## PROPAGATION VERSUS REVELATION

Let's define *propagation* and *revelation*. *Propagation* defines a messenger who proclaims a message, as in a pastor or evangelist proclaiming the gospel. *Revelation* is a supernatural removal of a barrier to see what was not known. The Book of Revelation is the removing of a veil so that the eyes of John could see the future of the church.

Gentiles come to Christ by the propagation of the gospel. I have preached in auditoriums, churches, cathedrals, football stadiums, and to a massive audience in Nigeria of more than three million in the open air. When you preach the gospel to Gentiles, it is common that hundreds and often thousands respond to the invitation to receive Christ. This is the power of the gospel and the message of proclaiming the truth of Jesus Christ as Lord and Savior.

This is not true of the Jewish people, who have been judicially blinded to the identity of Messiah. This is confirmed by David, whom Saint Paul quotes in Romans 11:10:

Let their eyes be darkened so that they do not see...

The more accurate translation of this verse is, "Let them be judicially blinded that they may not see."

So how do Jewish people from the time of Christ until today come to recognize the true identity of Christ? The answer is that those who recognize Christ as Messiah do so through divine revelation, as did the twelve disciples who followed Christ (Matt. 13:11) and the apostle Paul on the road to Damascus.

Let's go back to Matthew 13 where Jesus is teaching the Jewish people in parables. The disciples asked Christ why He was teaching the Jewish people in parables.

Christ answers: "Because it has been given to you [the disciples] to know the mysteries of the kingdom of heaven [revelation], but to them it has not given" (v. 11).

The point is made very clearly that Jewish people who come to recognize Jesus as Messiah do so by the process of divine revelation from God. However, it's imperative that all spiritual truth be established by two or more witnesses within the Word of God. Scripture should always be interpreted by scripture so that divine truth does not become corrupted by carnal knowledge or by personal bias.

The spiritual principle is that Jewish people today come to recognize Jesus Christ via revelation. Is there another witness, other than Jesus Christ in Matthew 13?

Yes—the conversion of Saint Paul in Acts, chapter 9. His name is

Saul as the drama of Acts 9 opens. He was born in the city of Tarsus, as confirmed by Acts 22:3. His birth occurred between A.D. 1 and A.D. 5. Saul grew up in a Greek culture and remained loyal to his Jewish roots all his life (Rom. 11:1; Phil. 3:5). His family was wealthy and socially influential (Acts 22:28), and they had the power as Jews to obtain Roman citizenship.

Paul was a Pharisee of Pharisees who received his education from the renowned teacher Gamaliel (Acts 22:3). Some theologians believe that at one time Saul must have been married, since marriage was required by the Pharisees to reach levels of promotion.

As the drama of Acts 9 opens, Saul has launched a vicious attack on the followers of Christ, having them thrown into prison to be beaten and murdered. As he comes near the gates of the city of Damascus, suddenly a bright light shone around him from heaven.

Saul had a dramatic face-to-face encounter with Jesus Christ, the light of the world. He was totally blinded physically by the experience for three days and was led by the hand like a child to the house of Ananias, who lived on the street called Straight.

Ananias laid his hands on Saul and prayed this prayer. Examine it closely!

> "Brother Saul, the Lord Jesus, who appeared on the road as you came, has sent me that you may receive your [physical] sight and be filled with the Holy Spirit." [Now listen to this!] Immediately, there fell from his eyes *something like scales* [the judicial blinding of God, spiritually, had ended], and he received his sight at once.
> —ACTS 9:17–18, EMPHASIS ADDED

Paul is yet another witness to the fact that Jewish people recognize Jesus the Messiah via revelation from God.

Just as Paul received the revelation of Christ as Messiah in Acts 9, there will be 144,000 Jewish witnesses in the Tribulation who have a similar experience, with 12,000 Jews from each tribe protected by the hand of God with a seal in their foreheads (Rev. 7:3). They shall cover the earth, bearing witness to their fellow Jews that they have had a supernatural visitation and now recognize Christ as Messiah.

Some organizations who target Jewish people for conversion use the phrase from Romans 1:16, which states, "to the Jew first," to justify their ministry. Let's look at that whole scripture and see what it really says:

> For I am not ashamed of the gospel of Christ, for it is the power of God to salvation for everyone who believes, for the Jew first and also for the Greek.
>
> —Romans 1:16

It's clear that the subject of this verse is the gospel of Christ.

The phrase "for the Jew first" is a matter of *sequence*—not preference. Paul is saying that the Word of God came to the Jews first, which is a fact of history. Later it came to the Gentiles. He confirms this in Romans 3:1–2, saying: "What advantage then has the Jew ...? Much in every way! Chiefly because to them were committed the oracles [Word] of God."

To say that God prefers to see the salvation of the Jews over Gentiles is to say that God is a "respecter of persons," which the Bible plainly denies. Romans 1:16 plainly states that the Word of God came to the Jewish people first as a matter of *sequence*—not preference.

# 16 GOD BLESSES GENTILES WHO BLESS ISRAEL

THE INABILITY OF the Jewish people to recognize Jesus as Messiah benefited the Gentiles by bringing to them the opportunity of salvation.

> I say then, have they stumbled that they should fall? Certainly not! But through their fall, to provoke them to jealousy, salvation has come to the Gentiles. Now if their fall is riches for the world, and their failure riches for the Gentiles, how much more their fullness!
>
> —ROMANS 11:11–12

The salvation of the Gentiles was intended by God to "provoke the Jews to jealousy," exciting them to seek and claim a share in the blessings of the new covenant.[1]

In Luke chapter 7, a centurion's servant was healed by Rabbi Jesus of Nazareth, who, being an observant Jew, would not enter the house of a Gentile. The Roman centurion asked the Jewish elders what he could do to get Jesus of Nazareth to enter his house and pray for his sick servant. The elders went to Jesus and pled with Him earnestly, saying that the Roman centurion deserved to be helped. (See Luke 7:1–10.) Why did he deserve to be helped?

The elders said to Jesus, "For he [the centurion] loves our nation, and has built us a synagogue" (v. 5).

The point is this: a practical act of kindness on the part of a Gentile provoked Jesus to enter the centurion's house to heal his sick servant, fulfilling Jesus' covenant with Abraham: "I will bless those that bless you..."

The tragedy of history has been that for two thousand years, recognized Christianity has not provoked Jews to jealousy by their kindness but has produced a harvest of hatred that caused the Jewish people to recoil in fear from those who waged war beneath the cross.

When the Roman Catholic Crusaders entered the city of Jerusalem in 1099, they trapped more than nine hundred Jewish women and children in their synagogue and burned them alive while they sang "Christ We Adore Thee." This kind of "Christianity" is no different from a member of the Taliban who straps himself with a bomb and murders Jews who refuse to believe in Islam.

In the twentieth century, six million Jews were systematically slaughtered by Adolf Hitler. Hitler and his Nazi monsters were never even slightly scolded by the pope, let alone excommunicated from the church for their crimes against humanity.

It's time for Christianity to reach out to our Jewish brothers and sisters, demonstrating the unconditional love of God, which is what Saint Paul commanded in Romans 15:27:

> For if the Gentiles have been partakers of their spiritual things [the Jews], their duty [the Gentiles] is also to minister to them [the Jewish people] in material things.

What riches came to the Gentiles because the Jewish people stumbled over the stumbling stone, which was Jesus of Nazareth?

## RICHES FOR THE GENTILE BELIEVER

- As Gentiles, we receive the unsearchable riches of the gospel of Jesus Christ.

- We receive the riches of the blessings of Abraham, which know no measure and have no limit.

- We receive the riches of faith by which the treasures of heaven are made possible to each of us.

- We receive the riches of repentance through which each of us becomes a child of God.

- We receive the riches of His love, joy, and eternal peace in the Holy Spirit.

- We receive the riches of salvation by grace through faith.

> • We receive the riches of adoption and the riches of being heirs and joint heirs with Jesus Christ.

The riches that came to the Gentiles because the Jewish people stumbled over the identity of Jesus Christ are without limit and beyond our knowing.

## LIFE FROM THE DEAD

For if their being cast away is the reconciling of the world, what will their acceptance be but life from the dead?

—ROMANS 11:15

Saint Paul is making a prediction that in Israel's future there will be a national spiritual resurrection that will be so dramatic it will be like someone coming back to life from the dead. How could such a thing happen? Remember, my friends, "With God all things are possible" (Matt. 19:26). How and when God will cause a spiritual resurrection to come to Israel is known only to God.

In Ezekiel 37, Ezekiel describes that very thing when God showed him the nation of Israel as a valley full of very dry bones. The bones were "very dry," meaning they had been dead a long time. Israel as a nation was dead for almost two thousand years. God commanded Ezekiel to prophesy to the dead bones. Ezekiel instantly obeyed the voice of the Lord, for obedience is better than sacrifice.

The valley of dry bones began to come together miraculously as Ezekiel spoke. Then came the sinews, the flesh, and skin, and those bones stood up an exceedingly great army. There is no doubt this is national Israel, for the scripture reads:

Son of man, these bones are the whole house of Israel.

—EZEKIEL 37:11

Israel is reborn and thrives today as a mighty democratic nation. We are now awaiting the Jewish people's spiritual resurrection. Ezekiel describes it as follows:

Then they [Israel] shall be My people, and I will be their God. David My servant shall be king over them, and they shall all have one shepherd; they shall also walk in My judgments and observe My statutes, and do them. Then they shall dwell in the land that I have given to Jacob My servant, where your fathers dwelt; and they shall dwell there, they, their children, and their children's children, forever; and My servant David shall be their prince forever. Moreover I will make a covenant of peace with them, and it shall be an everlasting covenant with them; I will establish them and multiply them, and I will set My sanctuary in their midst forevermore. My tabernacle also shall be with them; indeed I will be their God, and they shall be My people. The nations also will know that I, the LORD, sanctify Israel, when My sanctuary is in their midst forevermore.

—EZEKIEL 37:23–28

Count on it! God's love for Israel and the Jewish people is boundless for the patriarchs' sake. This spiritual awakening, which is very clearly predicted by Ezekiel, is now beginning and will soon explode into a global reality. It is God's time to pour out the spirit of grace upon the house of Israel and the Jewish people.

## THE JEWISH ROOT IS HOLY
## ROMANS 11:16

If the part of the dough offered as firstfruits is holy, then the whole batch is holy; if the root is holy, so are the branches.

—ROMANS 11:16, NIV

The Bible says, "Without holiness no one will see the Lord" (Heb. 12:14, NIV). The Word of God is saturated with the concept of holiness. Our Bible is called the *Holy Bible*. Jerusalem is called the Holy City. When we gather in the house of the Lord, we are on holy ground. The anointing oil that breaks every yoke is called the holy anointing oil. The tabernacle has the holy of holies where God Himself visited ancient Israel. The angels around the throne of God at this very moment are shouting in thunderous union, "Holy, holy, holy," night and day.

In Romans 11:16, Paul captures that theme, saying that if the initial dough that makes the loaf of *challah* bread is holy, the whole loaf is holy. The concept was given to Israel first in Numbers 15:20–21, describing a small "cake" baked from dough set aside for God. All bread baked thereafter from the "holy dough" made the whole loaf holy.

Paul uses the same principle and applies it to an olive tree, which is the symbol of Israel. Paul states, "If the root is holy, so are the branches."

The root of the olive tree is Abraham, Isaac, and Jacob. In Romans 11:28, Paul clearly states that Israel is "beloved for the sake of the fathers." The "fathers" are the patriarchs Abraham, Isaac, and Jacob.

Now follow Paul's transition. If the roots are holy (Abraham, Isaac, and Jacob), the branches are holy (v. 16). Who are the branches growing from the holy root? These branches are the righteous Jews, but not necessarily every Jew.

Note that in verse 17, "Some of the branches were broken off." This means that some individual Jews have been disciplined by God and are temporarily broken off (v. 23). Logic states that if some of the branches are broken off, some of the branches are still attached to the tree, and they are holy. Paul very clearly states that the Jewish people are still God's people and are considered by God to be holy.

## THE WILD OLIVE TREE
## ROMANS 11:17–24

Paul now turns his attention to the Gentiles. He writes:

> And you [Gentiles], being a wild olive tree, were grafted in among them [the Jewish people], and with them became a partaker of the root and fatness of the olive tree, do not boast against the branches. But if you do boast, remember that you do not support the root, but the root supports you. You will say then, "Branches were broken off that I might be grafted in." Well said. Because of unbelief they were broken off, and you stand by faith. Do not be haughty, but fear. For if God did not spare the natural branches, He may not spare you either. Therefore consider the goodness and severity of God: on those who fell, severity; but toward you, goodness, if you continue in His goodness. Otherwise you also will be cut off. And they also, if they do not continue in unbelief, will be grafted in, for God is able to graft them in again. For if you were cut out of the olive tree, which is wild by nature, and were grafted contrary to nature into a cultivated olive tree, how much more will these,

who are natural branches, be grafted into their own olive tree?

—ROMANS 11:17–24

Let's review the spiritual anatomy of this olive tree Paul is presenting.

First, its roots are the patriarchs Abraham, Isaac, and Jacob. The branches that have been broken off are generations of unbelieving Jews, and the branches that have been "grafted in" are the believing Gentiles. Please remember that there are Jewish branches that are still attached to the olive tree.

Theologians debate that wild olive branches (Gentiles) cannot be grafted into a natural olive tree. While this is true as a fact of nature in horticultural science, Paul clearly states in verse 24 that the wild olive branch being grafted in is "contrary to nature." This means the grafting in of the Gentiles is a supernatural act from the hand of God.

## A WARNING TO THE GENTILES

Saint Paul begins addressing the Gentiles directly in verse 13 ("for I speak to you Gentiles"), and he continues speaking to them until verse 25. In verses 17–22, he warns the Gentiles not to boast against Judaism because of the favor God has given to the Gentiles for the time being.

The Gentiles did not seek God, yet they now get to have a full share of the riches of Abraham. The transplanted olive branches "share the richness" of the olive tree.

What should the attitude of Gentiles be toward the Jewish people? Paul commands all Gentile believers of every generation, "Do not boast against the branches" (v. 18). Should you in your arrogance and pride be tempted to boast of the favor that God has given to you as a Gentile? You must remember that the Jewish root is bearing them, not them the root (v. 18). The Gentiles do not give life to the tree, but they draw life from the tree, which receives its life source from the taproot, which is Jewish, being Abraham, Isaac, and Jacob.

Then Paul allows the imaginary Gentile person to voice his opinion in verse 19, saying, "Branches were broken off that I might be grafted in." This very claim is made by those who teach that the church has replaced Israel in the economy of God. Replacement theologians teach that Israel has no role in the future of God's work. Their time is past, they teach; now we (the Gentiles) are the people of God. This teaching is false doctrine!

Paul makes it very clear the root of the tree is Jewish, and many natural branches (Jewish people) are yet attached to the olive tree. Israel has a prominent and equal place in the economy of God forever. Paul's description demolishes replacement theology, specifically in Romans 11:1 and 11, saying it is not true.

Paul then reminds any arrogant Gentile Christian, "Don't think high thoughts. Be afraid!" (See verse 20). Why be afraid?

Christians should fear because, "If God did not spare the natural branches [the Jewish people], He may not spare you either" (v. 21). The language in the Greek here is bold and forceful. Paul uses the word *kata phusis* (natural) and *para phusis* (unnatural) in Romans 11:24. The point is shocking, yet unmistakable. The Jewish people are natural to God, and the Gentiles are unnatural branches in God's economy.

Paul's use of the word *spare* recalls Romans 8:32: "He [God] who did not spare His own Son." Abraham, acting under God's command, was willing not to spare Isaac, but to offer him as a sacrifice to prove his absolute loyalty to God.

Is it too much to believe that Saint Paul is once more making a connection between Jewish people who had the first claim to "sonship" (Rom. 9:4) and Jesus Christ on the cross? If God did not spare His first son, Israel, and His only begotten Son, Jesus Christ, He certainly will judge arrogant Gentiles as severely as He judged the Jews who disobeyed the Torah. That's why Paul says to Gentile believers, "Do not be haughty [toward the Jewish people], but fear" (Rom. 11:20). Remember the words that God gave to Abraham: "I will bless those who bless you, and I will curse him who curses you" (Gen. 12:3).

## GOD'S FUTURE FOR HIS CHOSEN PEOPLE
## ROMANS 11:23–24

And they also, if they do not continue in unbelief, will be grafted in, for God is able to graft them in again. For if you were cut out of the olive tree which is wild by nature, and were grafted contrary to nature into a cultivated olive tree, how much more will these, who are natural branches, be grafted into their own olive tree?

—ROMANS 11:23–24

Most of Romans 11 deals with God's purposes for the Jewish people in this present age. Romans 11:1 deals with the fact God has not cast away the Jewish people in this present age. Romans 11:5 states, "Even so then, at this present time there is a remnant according to the election of grace." God has divinely chosen Jewish people at this present time who live in God's favor.

In Romans 11:30–31, Paul is referring to the salvation of the Jewish people at some point in the future.

Paul makes it clear in Romans 11:25 that Israel's blindness to the identity of Messiah will end when "the fullness of the Gentiles has come in." The fullness of the Gentiles will endure until Christ returns to earth. Then Paul plants the blockbuster verse of all the Book of Romans: "All Israel will be saved" (v. 26).

Notice the pattern of progression in Romans 11 concerning the redemption of the Jewish people in the future.

### PATTERN OF THE FUTURE FOR THE JEWS

- The *possibility* that the Jewish people could be grafted in at some point in the future: "God is able to graft them in again" (v. 23).

- The *probability* that the Jewish people will come to redemption in the future: "How much more will these, who are natural branches [the Jewish people], be grafted into their own olive tree?" (v. 24).

- The *absolute fact* that, at a time in the future, redemption will come to all righteous Jews: "And so all Israel will be saved" (v. 26).

Paul again presents God as a Creator who calls into being that which did not exist and raises the dead to life. There is the connection between the birth of the Jewish people and Isaac, whose parents were "as good as dead." Remember, Abraham and Sarah were sterile in their old age when Isaac, the son of promise, was born.

Now Paul presents the regeneration of the Jewish people from the "remnant according to the election of grace." Paul cups his hands to his mouth and shouts for all generations to hear, *"Am Israel Chai,"* meaning, "The people of Israel are alive."

Paul begins to summarize his argument by reminding his Gentile readers once more not to be arrogant toward the Jewish people because of the Gentiles' present favor with God. The Gentiles do not know it, but they are involved in a mystery, which is something else all together different than a problem.

A *problem* is something human intelligence can eventually work out. Problems are chess moves, crossword puzzles, and broken marriages. But a *mystery* is something that, when the answer is known, human intelligence cannot fully grasp its meaning.

## THE MYSTERY OF ISRAEL'S FUTURE
## ROMANS 11:25

> For I do not desire, brethren, that you should be ignorant of this mystery, lest you should be wise in your own opinion, that blindness in part has happened to Israel until the fullness of the Gentiles has come in.
>
> —ROMANS 11:25

There are seven mysteries of God in Scripture. They are as follows:

### THE SEVEN MYSTERIES OF GOD

1. The mysteries of the kingdom of God (Matt. 13:11)
2. The mystery of the olive tree (Rom. 11:25)
3. The mystery of Christ and the church (Eph. 5:32)
4. The mystery of piety (1 Tim. 3:16)
5. The mystery of the rapture of the church (1 Cor. 15:51)
6. The mystery of lawlessness (2 Thess. 2:7)
7. The mystery of God finished (Rev. 10:7)

A mystery in Scripture concerning a future event can be known only through divine revelation. These seven mysteries recorded in Scripture are explained, and they should be known by the body of Christ. Yet they are strangely ignored by the vast majority of Christians.

The specific mystery Paul is writing about here is that "all of Israel will be saved." Why is it a mystery? Obviously, no one could have predicted this in Paul's era without divine revelation. There are theologians today who can literally see the physical restoration of national Israel before their natural eyes, and still they deny that God has or will restore Israel.

Paul now shares with his Gentile readers that the "hardening" of Israel is only partial and temporary. It will last only until the full number of Gentiles come in (Rom. 11:25). Paul is using almost the exact words of Jesus, who said, "Jerusalem will be trampled by Gentiles until the times of the Gentiles are fulfilled" (Luke 21:24).

Paul's expectation that "all Israel will be saved" was exactly like Abraham and Sarah contemplating the birth of Isaac when they were totally barren. Yet Paul's revelation is not based on human possibility, but in "God, who gives life to the dead and calls those things which do not exist as though they did" (Rom. 4:17).

The fact of Scripture is this: at some point in the near future, there is going to be a massive spiritual awakening in Israel that will shock the world, and the Word of God will come true—"All Israel will be saved."

Could it be during Ezekiel's war as described in Ezekiel 38 and 39? Is this national spiritual awakening of Israel what Ezekiel refers to in Ezekiel 39:22, 29?

> "So the house of Israel shall know that I am the LORD their God from that day forward.... And I will not hide My face from them anymore; for I shall have poured out My Spirit on the house of Israel," says the Lord GOD.

# ALL ISRAEL WILL BE SAVED

THE OLD TESTAMENT is God's will concealed. The New Testament is God's will revealed. As you study Paul's writings, you discover that he makes a statement of faith and then supports it with Old Testament facts.

> And so all Israel will be saved, as it is written:
>
> "The Deliverer will come out of Zion,
> And He will turn away ungodliness from Jacob;
> For this is My covenant with them,
> When I take away their sins."
>
> —ROMANS 11:26–27

Paul's statement "All Israel will be saved" is taken from Isaiah 59:20–21, which reads in the Septuagint translation, "And the deliverer shall come for Zion's sake, and shall turn away ungodliness from Jacob. And this shall be my covenant with them, said the Lord."[1]

Paul's statement "All Israel will be saved" is also influenced by Psalm 14:7: "Oh, that the salvation of Israel would come out of Zion! When the LORD brings back the captivity of His people, let Jacob rejoice and Israel be glad."

Once more, the text speaks of a return. But this time it speaks of deliverance: "The salvation of Israel would come out of Zion."

Who is this deliverer from Zion?

I believe Saint Paul, Isaiah, and King David speak of Jesus of Nazareth. Here's my evidence, aside from the plethora of scriptures I've already given comparing Moses and Jesus Christ.

Zechariah writes: "They [those alive in Israel at that time] will look on me, the one they have pierced, and they will mourn for him as one mourns for an only child" (Zech. 12:10, NIV).

This is an amazing prophecy that clearly reveals who is this "deliverer out of Zion."

The word *pierced* in Zechariah 12:10 comes from the Hebrew word *daqar*, which means, "to thrust through with sword or spear," whereas in Psalm 22:16, the Hebrew *'ariy* is used: "They pierced My hands and My feet."

The Bible foretells that the "deliverer out of Zion" will be pierced in two ways: the piercing of hands and feet in crucifixion (prophesied centuries before crucifixion was known) and the piercing with sword or spear to the death, which was not normally a part of crucifixion. However, Jesus of Nazareth endured this second piercing. Therefore, Jesus Christ of Nazareth is the only man who has ever walked across the stage of human history who could be "the deliverer out of Zion."

Saint Paul now brings his long and complex argument to a close (Rom. 11:28–32). The Jewish people, the most brilliant race of people on the face of the earth, who were judicially blinded to the identity of Messiah, are now "enemies for your sake" (v. 28). Paul stated earlier in Romans 5:10 concerning the Gentiles that "we were enemies" of God because we were in rebellion to the will of God.

Paul qualifies the word *enemies* immediately with "for your sake." The Gentiles have benefited from Israel's partial and temporary blindness to Messiah, giving us the unsearchable riches of the gospel and the opportunity to come to repentance and redemption.

Briefly stated, the Jewish response to the gospel message has placed in the hands of the Gentiles the golden key that unlocked the door to the unsearchable riches of the kingdom of God. We, who were "outside the covenant, without hope and without God" have been made heirs and joint heirs. We have been grafted into the olive tree even though we were wild branches, which required a miraculous, supernatural grafting to make us one with God the Father.

Paul emphatically reminds his Gentile readers, "They [the Jewish people] are beloved for the sake of the fathers," meaning Abraham, Isaac, and Jacob. Inasmuch as both Gentiles and Jews are grafted into the olive tree of Romans 11, we therefore should remember that we are brothers and sisters in the kingdom of God and should treat each other with mutual respect reflecting this relationship.

In Pauline logic, the good deeds of the patriarchs built up merit with God from which future generations could draw. God's eternal loyalty to the Jewish people has to do with the patriarchs' loyalty to God and God's loyalty to His covenants to the Jewish people (Rom. 11:29).

Paul then says to Gentiles:

> For as you were once disobedient to God, yet have now obtained mercy through their disobedience, even so these also have now been disobedient, that through the mercy shown you they also obtain mercy.
>
> —ROMAN 11:30–31

Paul concludes the chapter praising the glory and wisdom of God, whose ways are past finding out. "For of Him and through Him and to Him are all things" (v. 36). God is the source, the sustainer, and the goal of all that exists. "...to whom be glory forever. Amen" (v. 36).

## CONCLUSION
## REVIEWING ROMANS 9–11

1. Romans 9–11 is, in fact, a theological codicil, a stand-alone document, reflecting God's position on the Jewish people after the cross.

2. Romans 9–11 is written exclusively concerning the Jewish people, as validated by eight textual statements in Romans 9:4–5.

3. God has chosen a remnant of surviving Jews "according to the election of grace." This election process is evidenced in Ishmael and Isaac, Jacob and Esau, in Pharaoh, and finally in the clay pot that has zero ability to tell the master potter what it shall become or the finished product of honor or dishonor it shall become.

4. Israel has not been cast away or put aside in the economy of God, as evidenced in Romans 11:1 and 11, clearly stating Israel has not been rejected of God. God's picture of Abraham's seed as being the stars of the heaven, representing the church, and the sand of the sea, which represents the

Jewish people, clearly states that Israel is eternal. The 144,000 are chosen from Israel in Revelation 7. How can that be if Israel does not exist in the economy of God? The judgment of the nations is about Israel and how the nations of the world treated Israel. If Israel has no place in the economy of God, why would that be?

5. Not all Jews are lost at this present time, since some have been chosen by a sovereign God "according to the election of grace" (Rom. 11:5). Grace means you did nothing to deserve it. God, in His infinite mercy, has decided to choose you to be in His divine favor.

6. The doctrine of *divine election* applies to nations and not to individuals. A remnant of the Jewish people has been divinely elected, and when the Gentile era ends, "all Israel will be saved." "All Israel" is to be identified as all believing Gentiles and Jews as evidenced by the natural branches (the Jewish people) of the olive tree and the unnatural branches (the believing Gentiles) (Rom. 11:17–21).

7. The Jewish people, in part, have been blinded to the identity of Messiah temporarily until the full number of Gentiles have come in, and then shall "all Israel be saved" (Rom. 11:25–26).

8. The roots of Christianity are Jewish (Rom. 11:16), and the Jewish roots support Christianity (v. 18).

9. Gentiles are commanded by Saint Paul to beware of any spirit of anti-Semitism, any attitude of arrogance toward the Jewish people lest the judgment of God fall on them. If God did not spare the Jewish people of judgment for sin, He most assuredly will not spare the Gentiles (Rom. 11:20–22).

10. A deliverer shall come out of Zion and take away the sins and ungodliness of Jacob, meaning the Jewish people (Rom. 11:26). That "deliverer out of Zion" is none other than Jesus Christ of Nazareth. I believe my generation will live to see Him sitting on the throne of King David on the Temple Mount in the city of Jerusalem, bringing the Golden Age of Peace to the world. It's coming much sooner than you think!

# 18 FIVE BIBLE REASONS CHRISTIANS SHOULD SUPPORT ISRAEL

A MERICA IS AT the crossroads! Will we believe and obey the Word of God concerning Israel, or will we continue to equivocate and sympathize with Israel's enemies? Our president has vowed to act against terrorists and those who harbor them while pressing Israel not to retaliate against Palestinian terrorists, who are very much a part of the international terrorist network.

As I write this book, Israel has been forced to abandon the Gaza Strip. Sadly, the European Union, the United Nations, and even the Bush administration continue to push for the creation of a Palestinian state that, we are told, will live "side by side with Israel in peace."

Did you see on national television what the "citizens" of this future state did in the last twenty-four hours as Israeli troops withdrew from Gaza? "Mobs carrying Hamas and Islamic Jihad flags rampaged through Gaza looting, shooting guns in the air, and then burning Jewish synagogues to the ground. The frenzy wasn't completely unexpected given the culture of death that has prevailed in the Palestinian territory for years. Bodies had been exhumed from Jewish graves during the evacuation, because everyone knew that once the Palestinians were in control the graves would be desecrated. There has not been one word of condemnation of this behavior from Palestinian leader Mahmod Abbas.

"Secretary of State Condoleezza Rice, while congratulating both the Israelis and the Palestinians for 'their effective coordination,' sadly failed to mention the torching of the synagogues."[1]

Senior Hamas leader Mahmoud al-Zahar, in an interview with Arab newspaper *Asharq Al Awsat*, said, "We do not and will not recognize a state called Israel.... This land is the property of all Muslims in all parts of the world.... Let Israel die."[2]

Is this the rhetoric of someone who yearns to live side by side in peace and harmony with Israel? Is this the partner for peace Washington is forcing on Israel?

The cornerstone of this Middle East policy, the alleged Roadmap for Peace, is to divide the land of Israel to create a terrorist-ruled Islamic Palestinian state, whose stated objective is the destruction of Israel.

Here's the problem!

God promises to pour out His judgment on any nation that tries to divide up the land of Israel. Listen to the voice of God as it speaks through His prophet Joel.

> I will also gather all nations, and…enter into judgment with them there on account of My people, My heritage Israel, whom they scattered among the nations; they have also *divided up My land*.…Multitudes, multitudes in the valley of decision! For the day of the LORD is near in the valley of decision.
> —JOEL 3:2, 14, EMPHASIS ADDED

God's Word is very clear! There will be grave consequences for the nation or nations that attempt to divide up the land of Israel. God's love for Israel is expressed in the words of Zechariah: "He who touches you [Israel] touches the apple of His eye" (Zech. 2:8).

God continues expressing His love for Israel, saying, "I will bless those who bless you, and I will curse him who curses you" (Gen. 12:3). This is and has been God's foreign policy toward the Jewish people from Genesis 12 until this day. Any man or nation that persecutes the Jewish people or the State of Israel will receive the swift judgment of God.

At this very moment, America finds itself bogged down in an unprovoked, worldwide war with radical Islamic terrorists with no end in sight. America is very vulnerable to terrorist attacks in the future, whose consequences could be much more severe than the three thousand lives lost on 9/11. This is not a time to provoke God and defy Him to pour out His judgment on our nation for being a principal force in the division of the land of Israel.

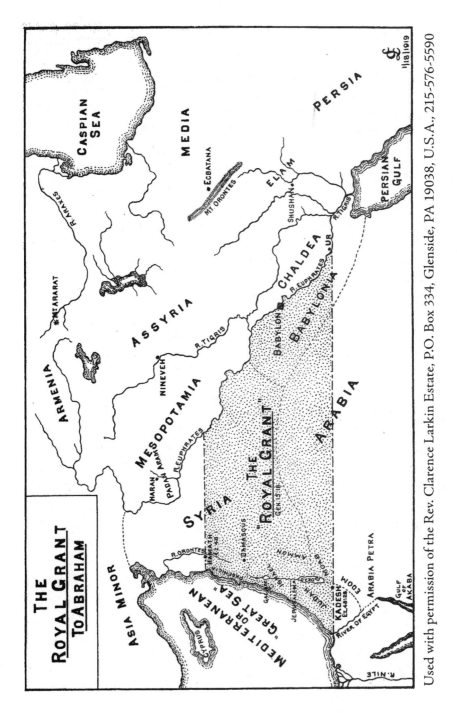

Used with permission of the Rev. Clarence Larkin Estate, P.O. Box 334, Glenside, PA 19038, U.S.A., 215-576-5590

## BIBLICAL REASONS

There are biblical reasons why America and all Bible-believing Christians must stand with Israel and their claim to the land.

### 1. Israel is the only nation created by a sovereign act of God.

Israel belongs to God himself! As Creator of heaven and earth (Gen. 1:1), God had the right of ownership to give the land to whomever He chose. God gave the title deed for the land of Israel to Abraham, Isaac, Jacob, and their descendants "forever" (Gen. 15:18; 17:2–8). Ishmael, father of Arabs, was excluded from the title deed to the land in Genesis 17:19–21. Therefore, modern-day Palestinians have no biblical mandate to own the land.

The boundaries of the State of Israel are recorded in Scripture. (See Numbers 34:2–15; Joshua 11:16–23; 13:1–22.) The boundaries are further described in Ezekiel 47:13–28 and all of chapter 48.

On the preceding page is a picture of the Royal Land Grant from God Almighty to Abraham, Isaac, Jacob, and their seed forever.[3]

When God established the nations of the world, He began with Israel. Israel is the center of the universe in the mind of God. (See Deuteronomy 32:8–10; Numbers 34:10–15; Joshua 11:16–22.)

### 2. Christians owe a debt of eternal gratitude to the Jewish people for their contributions, which gave birth to the Christian faith.

Paul recorded in Romans 15:27, "For if the Gentiles have been partakers of their [the Jews] spiritual things, their duty is also to minister to them in material things."

Jesus Christ, a prominent rabbi from Nazareth, said, "Salvation is of the Jews" (John 4:22). Consider what the Jewish people have given to Christianity;

- The sacred Scripture
- The prophets
- The patriarchs
- Mary, Joseph, and Jesus of Nazareth
- The twelve disciples
- The apostles

It is not possible to say, "I am a Christian," and not love the Jewish people. The Bible teaches that love is not what you say, but love is what you do (1 John 3:18). Someone has said:

> A bell is not a bell until you ring it,
> A song is not a song until you sing it,
> Love in your heart is not put there to stay,
> Love is not love until you give it away.[4]

### 3. Jesus never denied His Jewishness.

While some Christians try to deny the connection between Jesus of Nazareth and the Jews of the world, Jesus never denied His Jewishness. He was born Jewish. He was circumcised on the eighth day in keeping with Jewish tradition. He had His Bar Mitzvah on His thirteenth birthday. He kept the Law of Moses. He wore the prayer shawl Moses commanded all Jewish men to wear. He died on the cross with an inscription over His head, "King of the Jews."

Jesus considered the Jewish people His family. Jesus said, "Verily I say unto you, Inasmuch as ye have done it unto one of the least of these my brethren [the Jewish people...Gentiles were never called His brethren], ye have done it unto me" (Matt. 25:40, KJV).

### 4. Christians are to support Israel because it brings the blessings of God to them personally.

In Psalm 122:6, King David commands all Christians, "Pray for the peace of Jerusalem: May they prosper who love you." The scriptural principle of personal prosperity is tied to blessing Israel and the city of Jerusalem.

Why did Jesus Christ go to the house of Cornelius in Capernaum and heal his servant who was ready to die? Jesus went because the Gentile centurion deserved the blessing of God because he had demonstrated his love for the Jews by building a synagogue in Israel (Luke 7:5). When you do things to bless the Jewish people and the State of Israel, God will bless you.

Why did God the Father select the house of Cornelius in Caesarea to be the first Gentile house in Israel to receive the gospel? The answer is given repeatedly in Acts 10.

Acts 10:2 says: "...a devout man [Cornelius] and one who feared God with all his household, who gave alms generously to the people, and prayed to God always." Who were the people to whom Cornelius gave these alms? They were the Jewish people that lived around him.

Acts 10:4 states: "Your prayers and your alms have come up for a memorial before God."

Acts 10:31 reads: "...your alms are remembered in the sight of God."

The point is made three times in the same chapter. A righteous Gentile who expressed his unconditional love for the Jewish people in a practical manner was divinely selected by heaven to be the first Gentile house to receive the gospel of salvation and the first to receive the outpouring of the Holy Spirit.

These combined Scriptures verify that prosperity (Gen. 12:3; Ps. 122:6), divine healing (Luke 7:1–5), and the outpouring of the Holy Spirit (Acts 10) came first to Gentiles who blessed the Jewish people and the nation of Israel in a practical manner. Paul expands on this teaching in Romans 15:27.

The Bible principle for Gentiles being blessed for blessing the Jewish people could be seen with Jacob and Laban. Jacob, one of the patriarchs, worked for Laban, who was a Syrian. Laban changed Jacob's wages ten times, each time to his hurt. Jacob became weary with the abuse and told Laban he was leaving. Laban responded apologetically: "Please stay...for I have learned by experience that the LORD has blessed me for your sake" (Gen. 30:27). Laban was a Gentile who confessed that he recognized God's specific blessing to him and his family because of Jacob.

The blessing continues in the story of Joseph and Pharaoh. Joseph saved the Gentile world from starvation through his divine power to interpret dreams. Pharaoh blessed Joseph by making him the prime minister of the nation and by giving to his family the rich farm lands of Goshen, which were the best in Egypt. Pharaoh treated Joseph and the Jewish people as an extension of his own family. During this era in Egypt's history, the pyramids were built and the glory of Egypt reached its absolute pinnacle. Through the genius of Joseph, the food in storage was used to buy vast amounts of real estate for Pharaoh and Egypt.

Then there arose a pharaoh who did not know Joseph. That pharaoh persecuted the Jewish people. He made their lives grievous and difficult on purpose. The Jews were forced to make bricks without straw. They were beaten with whips, they were starved, and their male children were drowned in the Nile River.

God brought to that pharaoh and his administration ten plagues that destroyed the economy of the nation. In its finality, the firstborn in every Egyptian home died, and the pharaoh himself became bloated fish food, floating face down before the Jewish people who had been liberated from Egypt's bondage by walking through the Red Sea on dry ground.

It is to be noted that what a nation does to the Jewish people, God will do exactly the same to them. The Egyptians killed Jewish children in the Nile River. God sent a plague that killed the firstborn of every house in Egypt without the lamb's blood on the door. The tears of the Egyptians matched every Jewish tear to the last drop.

When I went to West Berlin in 1984 as a guest of the U.S. military to speak in their annual week of spiritual renewal, I was taken by a German tour guide through Checkpoint Charlie into East Berlin. What a contrast between capitalism and Communism. West Berlin was an oasis of boundless abundance created by the risk and reward system of capitalism. East Berlin was a barren desert with nothing to offer but empty promises. East Berlin was a poster child for Communism.

Separating East and West Germany were two ten-feet-high barbed-wire fences with a no-man's-land of one hundred yards filled with machine gun towers and German shepherd attack dogs. The German tour guide turned to me and fired a question I did not see coming: "Pastor Hagee, why did God allow the Russians to build fences around the German people, with machine guns and attack dogs?"

The answer flashed out of my mouth like lightening: "God allowed the Russians to build barbed-wire fences around the German people to hold you as prisoners with machine guns and German shepherd attack dogs because the German people did exactly the same thing to the Jews at every death camp. You did this at Dachau and Auschwitz, and for every Jew who died, you will have to answer to God."

199

**5. God judges the Gentiles for their abuse of the Jews.**

In Exodus 17, there's the story of the Amalekites, who attacked the children of Israel as they came up out of Egypt en route to the Promised Land. Because the Amalekites, who were descendants of Esau, whom God hated, attacked the Jewish people, God promised to be at war with Amalek from generation to generation.

> Then the LORD said to Moses, "Write this for a memorial in the book and recount it in the hearing of Joshua, that I will utterly blot out the remembrance of Amalek from under heaven." And Moses built an altar and called its name The-LORD-Is-My-Banner; for he said, "Because the LORD has sworn: the LORD will have war with Amalek from generation to generation."
> —EXODUS 17:14–16

Because Amalek attacked the Jewish people as they came up out of Egypt, God promised to be at war with him until He drove his remembrance from beneath the sun. That meant God intended to exterminate him and his people. Hundreds of years later, God was still at war with Amalek. God commanded King Saul to destroy the Amalekites utterly. We read:

> Thus says the LORD of hosts: "I will punish Amalek for what he did to Israel, how he ambushed him on the way when he came up from Egypt. Now go and attack Amalek, and utterly destroy all that they have, and do not spare them. But kill both man and woman, infant and nursing child, ox and sheep, camel and donkey."
> —1 SAMUEL 15:2–3

In 1 Samuel 15:28, because Saul refused to obey the Lord, God took the kingdom from him and gave it to another. The judgment on Saul was instantaneous, because he refused to carry out God's judgment against those who had attacked the Jewish people.

In 1 Samuel 15:28–29, Samuel said to Saul: "The LORD has torn the kingdom of Israel from you today, and has given it to a neighbor of yours [David], who is better than you. And also the Strength of Israel will not lie nor relent. For He is not a man, that He should relent."

There is a point here that cannot be missed. Hundreds of years passed from the time of Moses to King Saul, but God did not change

His mind about exterminating Amalek's descendants to the last "man, woman, infant and nursing child."

Another illustration of God judging the Gentiles who attacked the Jewish people was the pharaoh "that knew not Joseph."

A third illustration of God destroying Gentiles who attacked the Jewish people is that of Haman. Haman was an Old Testament Hitler who planned the first "final solution" for all the Jews living in Persia. The story is vividly recorded in the pages of God's Word. (See the Book of Esther.) The end result was that Haman and his seven sons hung from the gallows they built to hang the Jews of Persia upon. The judgment of God came to those who tried to bring destruction to the Jewish people. Exactly what Haman planned for the Jews happened to himself and his sons.

Where is the Roman Empire? Where are the Greeks? Where are the Babylonians? Where are the Turks? Where is the Ottoman Empire? Where are Adolf Hitler and his goose-stepping Nazis? They are all footnotes in the boneyard of human history, because they all made a common mistake. They attacked the Jewish people, and God Almighty brought them to nothing.

Hitler had Jews shot and thrown in death ditches and then burned. Others were gassed and burned in ovens, and their ashes filled the countryside like flakes of falling snow. How did Hitler die? He shot himself and ordered his fanatical lunatic Nazi followers to soak his body with fifty gallons of gas and then burn him to an ash. What you do to the Jews will happen to you.

God promises to punish the nations that come against Israel (Gen. 12:3). America, the Arabs, the European Union, the United Nations, Russia, China—indeed, all nations—are in the valley of decision. Every nation that presumes to interfere with God's plan for Israel, including the United States, stands not only against Israel but also ultimately against God. God is rising to judge the nations of the world based on their treatment of the State of Israel.

In March 2002, when White House rhetoric was moving against Israel, Senator James Inhofe (R-OK) gave one of the greatest speeches ever given on the floor of the United States Senate. Senator Inhofe titled his speech, "Seven Reasons Why Israel Is Entitled to the Land." Here is an abridged version of the senator's magnificent speech:[5]

1. *The archaeological evidence says it's Israel's land!*

    Every new archaeological dig supports the fact that the Jews have had a presence in Israel for three thousand years—including coins, cities, pottery, and other cultural artifacts. The Jewish claim predates the claim of any other people in the region. The ancient Philistines are extinct, as are other ancient peoples. They do not have the unbroken line the Israelis have. The first modern Israelis are direct descendants from the original Israelites.

2. *Israel has a historic right to the land.*

    Israel existed as a nation until the time of the Roman Empire. Even after the dispersions of A.D. 70 and A.D. 135, a strong Jewish presence remained. The Turks took control seven hundred years ago and ruled until they were defeated by Great Britain in World War I as allies of the Germans. British Field Marshall Edmond Allenby took Jerusalem without firing a shot. Grateful for the contributions Jewish scientists and businessmen had made to the war effort, Britain promised in 1917 to set aside certain captured lands (all present-day Israel and Jordan) for a Jewish homeland. There was no outcry over the plan because the land was considered worthless, unable to sustain any sizable population.

    Arabs began to repopulate the land only after the Jews reclaimed it and the land had begun to prosper. No nation in the region has a longer-standing historic claim to the land than Israel. Saudi Arabia was not created until 1913; Lebanon, 1920; Iraq, 1932; Syria, 1941; Jordan, 1946; and Kuwait, 1961.

3. *Israel's practical value to the Middle East*

    Israel is a marvel of modern agriculture. She has brought more food out of a desert than any other land. The Arabs should befriend Israel, import Israeli technology, and make the Middle East, like Israel, a food exporter.

    The Israeli Defense Forces bring to the troubled Middle East great stability. If the Israeli Defense Forces were not able to bring peace in the region, the United States of

America would need to commit thousands of troops at the cost of billions of dollars to secure a land that is critical to our national security inasmuch as the oil-rich Persian Gulf is at stake.

4. *Israel's land: the ground of humanitarian concern*

Six million Jews were slaughtered in Europe in World War II. Jews were persecuted in Russia under the czars, under Communism, and even now. For their own protection and development, the Jews need their homeland. If not there, where? The entire nation of Israel would fit into my home state of Oklahoma seven times.

5. *Israel is a strategic ally of the United States.*

Israel is an impediment to groups hostile to America. Were it not for our strategic ally, Israel, they would overrun the entire Middle East. We have only one friend in the region we can count on. Israel votes with us in the United Nations more than any other nation, including England, Canada, France, and Germany.

6. *Israel is a roadblock to terrorism.*

The war we face is not against a sovereign nation but against a fluid group of terrorists who move from one country to another. They are almost invisible. We need our alliance with Israel. If we do not stop terrorism in the Middle East, it will be on our shores. I believe the spiritual door was opened for an attack against the United States because the policy of our government has been to demand and pressure the Israelis not to retaliate in a significant way against terrorist strikes launched against them.

Since its independence in 1948, Israel has fought four wars: the War for Independence (1948–1949); the 1956 War, the Sinai Campaign; the Six-Day War in 1967; and the Yom Kippur War in 1973. In all four cases, Israel was attacked. They were never the aggressor. They won all four wars against impossible odds.

7. *We must support Israel's right to the land because God said so!*

In Genesis 13:14–17, the Bible says: "The LORD said unto

Abram...'Lift up now thine eyes, and look from the place where thou art...for all the land which thou seest, to thee will I give it, and to thy seed forever...'"

# ISRAEL—HISTORICAL TIMELINE

## THE FIRST COMMONWEALTH
### (CA. 1004–586 BCE)

1004      King David captures Jerusalem from the Jebusites. Makes Jerusalem the capital. (As some scholars point out, King David did not found Jerusalem, but conquered an already inhabited city that had been in existence for 2,000 years.)

1010–970 Reign of King David

CA. 960     King Solomon begins to build the first temple.

928       Division of kingdom into Israel (north) and Judah (south)

722       Assyrians conquer northern kingdom of Israel.

701       Hezekiah successfully withstands Sennacherib's attack on Jerusalem.

597       Babylonians capture Jerusalem.

586       Nebuchadnezzar destroys city and first temple and exiles Jews to Babylon.

## THE PERSIAN PERIOD
### (539–332 BCE)

539       Fall of Babylon

538–537 Cyrus allows Jews (about 50,000) to return to Jerusalem from Babylon.

520       Work begins on the building of the second temple under Zerubbabel.

515       Completion and rededication of the second temple

445       Nehemiah is appointed governor of Judea by Artaxerxes and rebuilds city walls.

397       Ezra the scribe initiates religious reforms.

## THE HELLENISTIC PERIOD
### (332–167 BCE)

332       Alexander the Great conquers Palestine.

323       Death of Alexander in Babylon; Wars of Succession begin.

320       Ptolemy I captures Jerusalem.

320–198 Rule of Egyptian Ptolemies

198–167 Rule of the Syrian Seleucids

167       Antiochus IV of Syria outlaws Juda and desecrates the second temple

## THE HASMONEAN PERIOD
### (167–63 BCE)

| | |
|---|---|
| 167–141 | Maccabean War of Liberation |
| 164 | Judah Maccabee recaptures Jerusalem and restores temple. |
| 166–160 | Rule of Judah the Maccabee |
| 160–143 | Rule of Jonathan |
| 143–135 | Rule of Simon Maccabeus |

## ROMAN PERIOD
### (63 BCE–324 CE)

| | |
|---|---|
| 63 | General Pompey and his Roman legions conquer Jerusalem. |
| 63–37 | Hasmonean rulers continue but under protection of Rome. |
| 40 | Rome appoints Herod king of Judea. |
| 40–4 CE | Reign of Herod the Great |
| 37 | King Herod captures Jerusalem. |
| 18 | Herod commences rebuilding of temple. |
| CA. 7 BCE–<br>31 CE | Life of Jesus of Nazareth |
| 4 BCE | Jerusalem is governed from Caesarea by Roman procurators. Herod dies. New Testament period under Roman rule (first century CE) |
| 26–36 | Pontius Pilate, Roman procurator of Judea |
| 27–31 | The ministry of Jesus |
| 31 | Crucifixion of Jesus |
| 63 | Temple completed |
| 66 | Jews revolt against the Romans. |
| 70 | Jerusalem is demolished by Titus; survivors are exiled or sold into slavery. |
| 132 | Bar Kochba leads a doomed revolt against Rome. |
| 135 | Emperor Hadrian rebuilds Jerusalem; builds new walls and renames the city Aelia Capitolina and country Palestine; bans Jews from Jerusalem. |

## BYZANTINE PERIOD
### (324–638)

| | |
|---|---|
| 313 | Emperor Constantine legalizes Christianity. |
| 324 | Constantine becomes sole ruler of the empire. |
| 326 | Queen Helena discovers Golgotha and other holy sites; her |

son, Constantine, builds the Anastasia (Church of the Holy Sepulcher).

| | |
|---|---|
| 438 | Empress Eudocia allows Jews to live in Jerusalem. |
| 614 | Persian conquest of Jerusalem |
| 628 | Emperor Heraculis recaptures the city. |

## EARLY MUSLIM PERIOD
### (639–1099)

| | |
|---|---|
| 638 | Six years after Muhammad's death, Caliph Omar captures Jerusalem; Jews readmitted. |
| 691 | Dome of the Rock is built by Caliph Abd Al-Malik. |
| 715 | Al-Aqsa mosque is completed by Al-Walid Al-Malik. |
| 750 | Power shifts from the Umayyads of Damascus to the Abbasids of Baghdad; Abbasids continue to enhance Jerusalem. |
| 969 | Fatimid conquest is soon followed by destruction of churches and synagogues. |
| 1071 | Seljuks devastate Jerusalem. |

## CRUSADER PERIOD
### (1099–1187)

| | |
|---|---|
| 1099 | Crusaders led by Godfrey de Bouillon capture Jerusalem; Baldwin I declared king; Jews and Muslims are slaughtered. |
| 1187 | Kurdish General Saladin captures Jerusalem from Crusaders; permits Jews and Muslims to return and settle in the city. |

## AYYUBID AND MAMLUK PERIOD
### (1187–1517)

| | |
|---|---|
| 1229 | Treaty returns Jerusalem to the Crusaders. |
| 1244 | Mamluk sultans defeat the Ayyubids and rule Jerusalem; city again in Muslim hands. |
| 1260 | Mamluks of Egypt rule Jerusalem from Cairo. |
| 1267 | Rabbi Moshe Ben Nahman arrives from Spain, revives Jewish congregation. |
| 1275 | Marco Polo stops in Jerusalem on his way to China. |
| 1291 | Acre, the last Crusader stronghold in the Holy Land, is captured by the Mamluks. |
| 1348 | Black Death plague hits Jerusalem. |
| 1492 | Jews arrive following Spanish Exile. |

## OTTOMAN PERIOD
### (1517–1917)

1517 Palestine and Jerusalem become part of the Ottoman Empire.

1537–1541 Sultan Suleiman the Magnificent rebuilds the city walls.

1799 Napoleon invades Palestine but does not try to conquer Jerusalem.

1831 Mohammed Ali of Egypt rules the country for nine years.

1838 First consulate (British) opens in Jerusalem.

1849 Consecration of Christ Church, first Protestant Church in the near east.

1860 First Jewish settlement outside walls of the city.

1892 Railroad connects the city to the coast.

1898 Visit by Dr. Theodor Herzl, founder of the World Zionist Organization

## THE BRITISH MANDATE PERIOD
### (1917–1948)

1917 British conquest and General Allenby's entry into Jerusalem

1920 The mandate for Palestine is conferred on Britain.

1921–1929 Arab-Jewish disturbances

1936–1939 Arab-Jewish disturbances

1925 Hebrew University buildings are inaugurated.

1947 United Nations resolution to create a Jewish and an Arab state in Palestine

1948 British withdraw from Palestine; the country is invaded by armies from neighboring states; the State of Israel is declared on May 14.

## THE ISRAELI PERIOD
### (1948–TO PRESENT)

1948–1949 Israel War of Liberation (also known as the "1948–1949 War")

1949 Israel-Transjordan Armistice Agreement signed; Jerusalem divided between two countries. Jerusalem is proclaimed capital of Israel; East Jerusalem is ruled by Jordan.

1967 Israelis capture old city during Six-Day War.

1973 The Yom Kippur War

1979 Egypt and Israel sign Peace Treaty.

1987 Beginning of Intifada

1993 Israel and the PLO sign the Declaration of Principles.

1995 Israel and Jordan sign Peace Treaty.[1]

# NOTES

### SECTION 1—WHERE ARE WE TODAY?

1. Amir Frayman, "Iran's Nuclear Program," *The Institute for Counter-Terrorism*, September 15, 2005, accessed at http://www.ict.org.il/ on October 5, 2005.

### CHAPTER 1—THE COMING NUCLEAR COUNTDOWN BETWEEN IRAN AND ISRAEL

1. Ahmed Rashid, "I've Sold Nuclear Secrets to Libya, Iran and North Korea," *Telegraph.co.uk*, as viewed at http://www.telegraph.co.uk/news/main.jhtml?xml=/news/2004/02/03/wpak03.xml on August 16, 2005.

2. Ibid.

3. Ibid.

4. Gil Hoffman and Tovah Lazaroff, "Iran Can Produce Nuclear Bomb by 2005," *Jerusalem Post*, August 5, 2003.

5. Kenneth Timmerman, *Countdown to Crisis* (New York: Crown Forum, 2005), 305.

6. Ibid., 305–306.

7. Interview with Gen. Paul Vallely (Ret.), *Executive Intelligence Review*, August 26, 2005, accessed at http://www.larouchepub.com/other/interviews/2005/3233paul_vallely.html on September 30, 2005.

8. Ibid.

9. Associated Press, "Israel Shares Intel With U.S. on Iran Nukes," *FoxNews.com*, accessed at http://www.foxnews.com/story/0,2933,153342,00.html on September 15, 2005.

10. Ibid.

11. "'Iran Is Close to a Nuclear Bomb': Iranian Scientist," *Iran Focus*, Wednesday, July 13, 2005, accessed at http://www.iranfocus.com/modules/news/print.php?storyid=2839 on September 15, 2005.

12. Ibid.

13. Graham Allison, *Nuclear Terrorism* (New York: Times Books, 2004).

14. Joel C. Rosenberg, "The Terror of Tehran," *National Review Online*, June 27, 2005, accessed at http://www.nationalreview.com/comment/rosenberg200506270949.asp on September 15, 2005.

15. Bret Baier, "What Are U.S. Military Options in Iran?" *FOXNews.com*, April 24, 2005, accessed at http://www.foxnews.com/story/0,2933,154245,00.html on September 15, 2005.

16. William M. Arkin, "Secret Plan Outlines the Unthinkable," *Los Angeles Times*, March 9, 2002, accessed at http://www.commondreams.org/cgi-bin/print.cgi?file=/views02/0309-04.htm on September 30, 2005.

17. Ibid.

18. Ibid.

19. Copyright AP/ Wide World Photos, used by permission.

20. Felix Frish, "How to Attack Reactors in Iran," *Ma'ariv*, April 19, 2005.

21. Ibid.

22. Ibid.

23. Ibid.

24. "Multinuclear Middle East—Iran, the Bomb and Israel," Strategic Dialogue Center Conference, Netanya Academic College, Israel, April 17, 2005.

25. David Wood, "U.S. to Sell Precision-Guided Bombs to Israel," Newhouse News Service, September 23, 2004, accessed at http://www .newhousenews.com/archive/wood092304.html on September 16, 2005.

26. Joyce Howard Price and David R. Sands, "Iran Leader Linked to '79 Embassy Crisis," *Washington Times*, June 30, 2005, accessed at http:// www.washingtontimes.com/world/20050630-124235-3835r.htm on August 26, 2005.

27. "Aljazeera: Mahmoud Ahmadinejad Involved in Planning U.S. Embassy Takeover and Lobbied for Takeover of Soviet Embassy," Hyscience.com, accessed at http://www.hyscience.com/archives/2005/06/ aljazeera_mahmo.php on August 26, 2005.

28. "French Daily: Iran's Ahmadinejad Was Key US Embassy Hostage-Taker," *Iran Focus*, June 29, 2005, accessed at http://www.iranfocus.com/ modules/news/article.php?storyid=2687 on August 26, 2005.

29. "Aljazeera: Mahmoud Ahmadinejad Involved in Planning U.S. Embassy Takeover and Lobbied for Takeover of Soviet Embassy."

30. Ramita Navai, "President Invokes New Islamic Wave," *Times Online*, June 30, 2005, accessed at http://www.timesonline.co.uk/ article/0,,251-1674547,00.html on August 26, 2005.

31. Safa Haeri, "Iran on Course for a Showdown," *Asia Times Online*, October 28, 2005, accessed at http://www.atimes.com/atimes/Middle_ East/GJ28Ak03.html on October 28, 2005.

32. Ibid.

33. Scott Peterson, "Iran's New Hard-Liner Maps Path," *Christian Science Monitor*, accessed at http://www.csmonitor.com/2005/0627/ p01s04-wome.html?s=widep on August 26, 2005.

34. Ali Akbar Dareini, "Iran Defies West, Resumes Nuclear Work," Associated Press, KansasCity.com, accessed at http://www.kansascity

.com/mld/kansascity/news/special_packages/election2004/polls/12330891
.htm?template=contentModules/printstory.jsp on October 18, 2005.

35. "Russia to Expand Nuclear Aid to Iran," *Washington Times,* July
27, 2002, accessed at http://nl.newsbank.com/nl-search/we/Archives?p_
product=WT&p_theme=wr&p_action=s on August 26, 2005.

36. "Iran Has Gas Type Used in Atom Bombs, Report Says," *Iran Focus,*
September 2, 2005, accessed at http://www.iranfocus.com/modules/news/
article.php?storyid=3578 on October 3, 2005.

37. Ibid.

38. "Bush Warns Iran on Nuclear Plans," *BBC News, World Edition,*
August 13, 2005, accessed at http://news.bbc.co.uk/2/hi/middle_
east/4147892.stm on August 26, 2005.

## CHAPTER 2—AN AMERICAN HIROSHIMA?

1. Baier, "What Are U.S. Military Options in Iran?"

2. "Senate Ready to Up War Aid," October 6, 2005, CBS News,
accessed at http://www.cbsnews.com/stories/2005/10/06/iraq/
main917420.shtml on October 7, 2005.

3. Baier, "What Are U.S. Military Options in Iran?"

4. Ibid.

5. Ibid.

6. Ibid.

7. Ibid.

8. Timmerman, *Countdown to Crisis,* 313–314.

9. "A Preemptive Attack on Iran's Nuclear Facilities: Possible
Consequences," CNS Research Story, Center for Nonproliferation Studies,
accessed at http://cns.miis.edu/pubs/week/040812.htm on September 30,
2005.

10. "Iran's 'Suicide Operations' Chief Vows to Hit U.S. Interests," *Iran
Focus,* August 23, 2005, accessed at http://www.iranfocus.com/modules/
news/article.php?storyid=3429 on October 3, 2005.

11. Ibid.

12. "Iran Offers Atomic Know-how to Islamic States," Reuters,
September 15, 2005, accessed at http://www.freerepublic.com/focus/
f-news/1484885/posts on September 30, 2005.

13. Ryan Mauro, "Paul Williams Details 'American Hiroshima,'"
*WorldNetDaily,* September 3, 2005, accessed at http://www.worldnetdaily
.com/news/article.asp?ARTICLE_ID=46127 on September 30, 2005.

14. Ibid.

15. Ibid.

16. Ibid.

17. Ibid.

18. Ibid.

19. Ibid.

20. Ibid.

21. "Iran Plans to Knock Out U.S. With 1 Nuclear Bomb," from Joseph Farah's G2 *Bulletin, WorldNetDaily,* April 25, 2005, accessed at http://worldnetdaily.com/news/article.asp?ARTICLE_ID=43956 on September 30, 2005.

22. "What Katrina Taught Iran," Joseph Farrah's *G2 Bulletin,* September 19, 2005, 1–5.

23. "Iran Plans to Knock Out U.S. With 1 Nuclear Bomb."

**CHAPTER 3—UNVEILING ISLAM**

1. "Islam in Iran," *Wickipedia,* accessed at http://en.wikipedia.org/wiki/Islam_in_Iran on September 16, 2005.

2. Dave Hunt, "A Moment for Truth," *The Berean Call,* October 2001, accessed at http://www.netanyahu.org/momentfortruth.html on October 3, 2005.

3. For a thorough discussion of the two seasons of Muhammad's life, see Mark A. Gabriel, *Islam and the Jews* (Lake Mary, FL: Charisma House, 2003), chapter 8.

4. Ibid., 46.

5. Ibid., 49.

6. *Jihad Watch,* October 5, 2005, accessed at http://www.jihadwatch .org/archives/2005/10/008438print.html on October 5, 2005.

7. Ibid.

8. Rod Dreher, "Islam According to Oprah," *Theology Online.com,* accessed at http://www.theologyonline.com/forums/showthread .php?t=7949 on October 3, 2005.

9. Ibid.

10. Samuel P. Huntington, *The Clash of Civilizations and the Remaking of World Order* (New York: Simon & Schuster, 1998).

11. "'Jihad in America' Video Is Here: PBS Documentary Reveals Domestic Terror Threat," *WorldNet Daily,* October 31, 2001, accessed at http://www.wnd.com/news/article.asp?ARTICLE_ID=25136 on October 12, 2005.

12. "All About Islam," SimpleToRemember.com, Judaism Online,

accessed at http://www.simpletoremember.com/vitals/IslamJudaism.htm on September 16, 2005.

13. Rabbi Moshe Reiss, "The Clash of Civilizations or Religions," *Bible Commentator: Islam and the West*, accessed at http://www.moshereiss.org/west/02_clash/02_clash.htm on September 16, 2005.

14. Ibid.

15. "Arab-Israeli Conflict: Basic Facts," Israel Science and Technology, accessed at http://www.science.co.il/Arab-Israeli-conflict-2.asp on September 16, 2005.

16. Joel Leyden, "Al-Qaeda, the 39 Principles of Holy War," Israel News Agency, accessed at http://www.israelnewsagency.com/Al-Qaeda.html on October 5, 2005.

17. Boaz Ganor, "Not One Jewish Village," International Policy Institute for Counter-Terrorism, accessed at http://www.ict.org.il/articles/islamic.htm on September 16, 2005.

18. Ibid.

19. Daniel Pipes, "The Danger Within: Militant Islam in America," *Commentary*, 2001, accessed at http://www.danielpipes.org/article/77 on October 3, 2005.

20. Ibid.

21. Reza Safa, *Inside Islam* (Lake Mary, FL: Charisma House, 1996).

22. Mark A. Gabriel, *Jesus and Muhammad* (Lake Mary, FL: Charisma House, 2004), 147.

23. Ibid., 143.

24. Ibid., 147.

25. Ibid., 151–152.

26. Article 11 of a 36-article covenant, "The Covenant of Hamas," outlining the position of Hamas, the largest, most active jihad group fighting in Israel, toward Israel; accessed at www.hraic.org/the_covenant_of_hamas.html on December 12, 2002, in Gabriel, *Islam and the Jews*, 150.

27. Abdullah Alnafisy, *No to Normalization With Israel*, 2nd ed. (Michigan: The Islamic Assembly of North America, 2000), in Gabriel, *Islam and the Jews*, 151.

## CHAPTER 4—JERUSALEM: THE CITY OF GOD

1. David Aikman, "For the Love of Israel," *Charisma*, August 1996, 66.

2. U.S. Department of State, "Roadmap for Peace in the Middle East," accessed at http://www.state.gov/r/pa/ei/rls/22520.htm on August 17, 2005.

3. For support of the atrocities committed during the siege of Titus,

including incidents of cannibalism, see "Roman Procurators," accessed at http://emp.byui.edu/HAYESR/papers/matt24.htm on August 17, 2005.

4. Derek Prince, *Promised Land* (Grand Rapids, MI: Chosen Books, 1982), 92–93.

## CHAPTER 5—THE WAR AGAINST THE JEWS

1. "Siloam Inscription and Hezekiah's Tunnel," Biblical Heritage Center, accessed at http://www.biblicalheritage.org/Places/hez-tun.htm on October 13, 2005.

## CHAPTER 6—THE RISE OF ANTI-SEMITISM

1. Aikman, "For the Love of Israel."

2. Malcolm Hay, *The Roots of Christian Anti-Semitism* (New York: Freedom Library Press, 1981), 13.

3. Josephus Flavius, *The New Complete Works of Josephus* (Grand Rapids, MI: Kregel Publications, 1999), 872–873.

4. Flavius, *The New Complete Works of Josephus.*

## CHAPTER 7—CENTURIES OF MISTREATMENT

1. "What Is Replacement Theology?" *Got Questions? The Bible Has the Answers,* accessed at http://www.gotquestions.org/replacement-theology .html on August 19, 2005.

2. Franklin Litell, *The Crucifixion of the Jews* (Macon, GA: Mercer University Press, 1996), 30.

3. John Hagee, *Should Christians Support Israel* (N.p.: Dominion Publishers, 1987), 5.

4. Dagobert R. Runes, *The War Against the Jews,* (New York: Philosophical Library, Inc., n.d.), 42. John Chrysostom, *Discourses Against Judaizing Christians,* translated by Paul W. Harkins. *The Fathers of the Church;* v. 68 (Washington: Catholic University of America Press, 1979)

5. "Invasions Under the Cross," Suppressed Histories.net accessed at http://www.suppressedhistories.net/secret_history/invasions_cross.html on September 23, 2005.

6. Elinor Slater and Robert Slater, *Great Moments in Jewish History* (New York: Jonathan David Publishers, 1998), 162.

7. Ibid.

8. Ibid., 163.

9. Elwood McQuaid, *The Zion Connection* (Eugene, OR: Harvest House, 1996), 17.

10. Slater, *Great Moments in Jewish History*, 166.

11. Runes, *The War Against the Jews*, 171.

12. Cecil Roth, *The Spanish Inquisition* (New York: W. W. Norton & Company, 1996); also see "The Spanish Inquisition," The Bible Study, accessed at http://www.bibletopics.com/biblestudy/64.htm on August 19, 2005.

13. Cecil Roth, *History of the Jews in England* (Glouchester, UK: Clarendon Pr, 1985).

14. Malcolm Hay, *The Roots of Christian Anti-Semitism* (New York: Freedom Library Press, 1981), 166.

15. *Encyclopedia Judaica*, volume 3 (Jerusalem, Keter Publishing House, 1978), 103.

16. Hay, *The Roots of Christian Anti-Semitism*, 169.

17. Adolf Hitler, *Mein Kampf*, translated by Ralph Manheim (Boston: Houghton Mifflin Co. 1971), 65; also Sid Roth, "The Constantine Conspiracy," Sid Roth's Messianic Vision: Jewish Roots, accessed at http://www.sidroth.org/jewishroots_main3.htm on August 19, 2005.

18. "Sixtieth Day, Friday, 15 February 1946, Morning Session: Nuremberg Trial Proceedings, Vol. 7," The Avalon Project at Yale Law School, accessed at http://www.yale.edu/lawweb/avalon/imt/proc/02-15-46.htm on October 13, 2005.

19. Hay, *The Roots of Christian Anti-Semitism*, 11.

20. Runes, *The War Against the Jews*, 13.

21. Ibid., 20.

22. Ibid., 91.

23. Harold Fickett, "John Paul II: Prophet of Freedom," GodSpy, Faith at the Edge, accessed at http://www.godspy.com/faith/John-Paul-the-Great-The-Prophet-of-Freedom-by-Harold-Fickett.cfm on September 23, 2005.

24. Sam Ser, "What Will Follow 'the Best Pope the Jews Ever Had'?", *Jerusalem Post*, April 3, 2005, accessed at http://www.jpost.com/servlet/Satellite?pagename=JPost/JPArticle/ShowFull&cid=1112494793946 on August 19, 2005.

25. Ibid.

26. Ibid.

## CHAPTER 8—JERUSALEM REGAINS INDEPENDENCE

1. "Modern History Sourcebook: The Balfour Declaration," accessed at http://www.fordham.edu/halsall/mod/balfour.html on August 23, 2005.

2. "The Palestine Mandate of the League of Nations, 1922," The British Mandate for Palestine, accessed at http://www.mideastweb.org/mandate .htm on August 23, 2005.

3. Menachem Begin, *The Revolt* (New York: Dell Publishing, 1951, 1978).

4. "The British White Paper of June 1922," The Avalon Project at Yale Law School, accessed at http://www.yale.edu/lawweb/avalon/mideast/ brwh1922.htm on August 23, 2005.

5. Begin, *The Revolt*, 70.

6. Ibid.

7. Ibid.

8. "The Bombing of the King David Hotel," Jewish Virtual Library, accessed at http://www.jewishvirtuallibrary.org/jsource/History/King_ David.html on August 23, 2005.

9. "Declaration of Israel's Independence, 1948," The Avalon Project at Yale Law School, accessed at http://www.yale.edu/lawweb/avalon/ mideast/israel.htm on August 23, 2005.

10. "How Did the Arab Territory of Transjordan Come Into Being?" Palestine Facts: British Mandate Transjordan, accessed at http://www .palestinefacts.org/pf_mandate_transjordan.php on August 23, 2005.

11. Slater, *Great Moments in Jewish History*, 115.

12. Ibid., 116.

13. Ibid.

14. Ibid., 116–117.

15. Ibid.

16. Ibid., 122.

17. Ibid., 126.

18. Ibid.

19. Ibid., 128.

20. Ibid.

21. Ibid.

### SECTION 3 —WHAT DOES THE FUTURE HOLD?

1. John Hagee, *The Battle for Jerusalem* (Nashville, TN: Thomas Nelson Publishers, 2001), 103–119.

### CHAPTER 10 —EZEKIEL'S WAR: THE RUSSIANS ARE COMING

1. *International Standard Bible Encyclopaedia*, Electronic Database 1996, Biblesoft.

2. Dean Stanley, *History of the Eastern Church*, out-of-print. See also Dan Styles, "Keeping Perspective When We Differ," accessed at http://www.tidings.org/editorials/editor200005.htm on August 30, 2005.

3. John Cumming, MD, *The Destiny of Nations* (London: Hurst & Blackette, 1864).

4. Hal Lindsey, *The Late Great Planet Earth* (Grand Rapids, MI: Zondervan, 1970), 59.

5. Vernon J. McGee, *Through the Bible*, vol. 3 (Nashville, TN: Thomas Nelson Publishers, 1982), 513.

6. Ibid., 513–514.

7. Wilhelm Gesenius, DD, *Hebrew and English Lexicon* (n.p.).

8. Jephraim P. Gundzik, "The Ties That Bind China, Russia and Iran," *Asia Times Online*, June 4, 2005, accessed at http://www.atimes.com/atimes/China/GF04Ad07.html on August 30, 2005.

9. "Iran Removes UN's Nuclear Seals," *BBC News*, UK edition, accessed at http://news.bbc.co.uk/go/pr/fr/-/1/hi/world/middle_east/4136662.stm on August 30, 2005.

## Chapter 11—The End of the Beginning

1. Alan Dershowitz, *The Case for Israel* (Hoboken, NJ: John Wiley & Sons, 2004).

2. For a brief look at the history and location of Petra, see http://www.brown.edu/Departments/Anthropology/Petra/ (viewed August 31, 2005).

3. Stephen Roach, "Blaming China," *Time Asia*, posted Monday, May 9, 2005, on AmericanEconomicAlert.org, accessed at http://www.americaneconomicalert.org/news_item.asp?NID=1529663 on October 14, 2005.

4. Mark Mazzetti, "Chinese Army Threaten Asia, Rumsfeld Says," *Los Angeles Times*, June 4, 2005, posted at GlobalSecurity.org, In the News, accessed at http://www.globalsecurity.org/org/news/2005/050604-china-asia.htm on August 31, 2005.

5. Peter S. Goodman, "Big Shift in China's Oil Policy," *Washington Post*, July 13, 2005, washingtonpost.com, accessed at http://www.washingtonpost.com/wp-dyn/content/article/2005/07/12/AR2005071201546_pf.html, on August 31, 2005.

6. "Armageddon," at Philologos, Bible Prophecy Research, accessed at http://philologos.org/bpr/files/a005.htm on August 31, 2005.

### CHAPTER 13—WHO IS A JEW?

1. John Toland, *Adolf Hitler* (New York: Anchor, 1991), 3–4.

### CHAPTER 16—GOD BLESSES GENTILES WHO BLESS ISRAEL

1. *Adam Clarke's Commentary*, Electronic Database. Copyright © 1996 by Biblesoft.

### CHAPTER 17—ALL ISRAEL WILL BE SAVED

1. *The Septuagint Version of the Old Testament*, with an English Translation by Sir Lancelot Brenton, accessed at http://www.ccel.org/b/brenton/lxx/htm/TOC.htm on September 23, 2005.

### CHAPTER 18—FIVE BIBLE REASONS CHRISTIANS SHOULD SUPPORT ISRAEL

1. Adapted from Gary L. Bauer press release on September 13, 2005, OurAmericanValues.org, accessed at http://www.ouramericanvalues.org/index.php.

2. From an interview with Hamas leader Dr. Mahmoud al-Zahar that appeared in *Asharq Al-Awsat* on August 18, 2005, accessed at http://memri.org/bin/articles.cgi?Page=archives&Area=sd&ID=SP96405 on September 23, 2005.

3. The Royal Grant to Abraham map was taken from Clarence Larkin, *Dispensational Truth* (Adrian, MI: Lifeline Books, 1918), available now from Rev. Clarence Larkin Estate at http://www.larkinestate.com/index.html.

4. This quote is attributed to Oscar Hammerstein II, who gave it as advice to Mary Martin.

5. Senate Floor statement by Senator James Inhofe, "Seven Reasons Why Israel is Entitled to the Land," March 4, 2002, *CBN.com* accessed at http://www.cbn.com/CBNnews/news/020308c.asp on September 23, 2005.

### APPENDIX: ISRAEL—HISTORICAL TIMELINE

1. Permission has been applied for from the History Channel, A&E Network.

# INDEX